as we grieve

discoveries
of grace in
sorrow

as we grieve

jan groft

GRAHAMHOUSE
books

All scripture quotations, unless otherwise indicated, are taken from the
HOLY BIBLE, NEW INTERNATIONAL VERSION®. NIV®. Copyright
©1973, 1978, 1984 by International Bible Society. Used by permission
of Zondervan. All rights reserved.

Excerpts from MOMENTS OF GRACE by Patricia Gaines, copyright
©1997 by Patricia Gaines. Used by permission of Crown Publishers, a
division of Random House, Inc.

From IN LIEU OF FLOWERS by Nancy Cobb, copyright ©2000 by
Nancy Howard Cobb. Used by permission of Pantheon Books, a division
of Random House, Inc.

The author also thanks *Central PA* Magazine and publisher WITF, Inc. for
permission to reprint portions of her essays entitled "Breathing for Elaine,"
which appeared in the August 1998 issue of that publication and
"Manolo's Drawings," which appeared in the May 2007 issue.

Published by Graham House Books
Lititz, Pennsylvania 17543
First Edition

Printed in the United States of America

Library of Congress Cataloging-in Publication Data

Groft, Jan.
As we grieve : discoveries of grace in sorrow / Jan Groft. -- 1st ed.
    p. ; cm.

ISBN 978-0-9842306-0-0

1. Grief. 2. Bereavement. 3. Loss (Psychology) 4. Short stories, American.
I. Title.

BF575.G7 G76 2010

155.937   2009909131

For Randy

And in memory of my mother

Josephine C. Coco

February 14, 1914—August 30, 2006

contents

acknowledgments

Many, many months ago, Lil Copan asked questions starting with the words "What if you…" which made me wonder, "But how?" Her prodding sparked an idea that prompted my search for the experiences of others, and for that I am grateful. Dozens of people generously shared and entrusted me with their stories. This book is their book; I hope I have done their memories justice.

Martha Barry, Bob Justice, Chris Noël and Francie Thayer responded to early drafts of my manuscript with sensitivity, honesty and wisdom. Their feedback enriched these pages.

Peg Marks encouraged me by asserting that she was going to "need" to read this book. And she listened. A lot.

Howard Rice kept me supplied with poems, friendship

and affirmation, as only Howard can do.

Marge Henderson and Pat Latshaw were and are always there for me.

Peter Latshaw ignited my entrepreneurial spirit, which we both garnered from the same source. Jim Corrigan was an amazing sounding board. His perceptiveness and generous insights inspired a deeper connection with my own work. Noah Martin kindly shared his valuable publishing experience.

The folks at Emerald Book Company/Greenleaf Book Group have proven to be competent and energetic. I thank them for sharing their expertise. Ditto to the team at EMSI.

Randy Groft, my partner both in creative endeavors and in life, gave generously and patiently of his design talent and support. Darcy, Scott, Katherine, Ruby and Macy continue to inspire me just by being who they are.

And the Creator of the mountains encouraged me—through that vista and in many other ways—to *keep going*.

"If God be for us,

who can be against us?"

Romans 8:31

one
embraced by
grace

an unexpected
embrace

I t was a scorcher of a Sunday in July, a day when the
air barely budged and hung heavy around my shoulders. I hated the thought of leaving my best friend
alone with her cancer, but Elaine's brown eyes were starting
to glaze, and she was too hospitable to sleep while I was
visiting. We had first met when our daughters were one-
year-olds splashing in baby pools back where our yards
joined. Since then, we'd shared secrets, trips to the beach,
disco dance lessons, not to mention numerous discussions
about Elaine's hair color. Most recently, her hair had been
dark brown and before that, blonde. Once it even turned
purple, which had her scurrying back to the hairdresser
only to be endowed with an interim shade of green. Now
on this hot summer day, though I had no way of knowing it at the time, we would say our final good-bye.

"Can I get you anything before I go?" I asked.

"My wig stand," she said.

Since the chemo had taken effect, and even since she'd insisted on stopping it, I'd never seen Elaine without the hairpiece, an effort, I believe, to ease her friends' pain even more than her own. Her forehead glistened with sweat, and I figured as soon as I left, she'd remove the wig. But when I returned to her family room with the stand, she was sitting with the ash brown locks in one hand, and with the other, she was scrubbing a napkin across her own sparse crop of hair, at last in its natural shade. I stopped and gazed at my friend.

"You're beautiful," I said, half-whispering. And she was, her fully exposed ears so delicate, her hair such a rich crimson-brown, that the sight of her left me breathless. All the things I knew about my friend of sixteen years rushed through me: her big heart, her flat-out truthfulness, her self-effacing humor, her unwavering friendship. A portrait so genuine and complete that it occurs to me now, looking back, that God was right there embracing me in my sorrow.

At the time, I don't believe my aching heart grasped the gift before me, but now I understand that is exactly what it was. Unexpected. Deeply touching. A memory that would return to me framed in magnanimous grace. The more I think about it, the more I see how often I have been blessed by these moments of light with which God imbues the darkness. The moments arrive quietly, not with a clap of thunder or a flurry of confetti. No, God displays class in gift-giving, subtly setting treasures out to be discovered.

This is a book about making that discovery. It is about finding God's love tucked into the unlikely folds of loss and grief, a companion on the journey through sorrow that most of us, sooner or later, will be called upon to make. Nurturing a heart open to recognizing God's presence instills hope. Like when a hospice patient opened her eyes from an afternoon nap, and before I could introduce myself as her volunteer visitor, she smiled and said, "I had the most wonderful day yesterday."

Or the moment I knelt beside my mother's casket. After a lifetime of relentless efforts to please her, that one gaze at the content expression on her face overwhelmed me with the realization that her happiness was never mine to cultivate in the first place. It is moments like these that make it feel as if God and I are doing a jitterbug—perfectly synchronized—just as when Mr. Shoemaker, my elementary school principal, played Elvis Presley records at indoor recess for us to dance to, and at a crescendo, my partner lifted me high into the air.

A clarity sets in when the recognition takes hold that

we are in communion with a power that transcends our own limited capabilities. In *Surprised by Joy*, C. S. Lewis describes it as "joy" or "romance," a notion that his friend Chad Walsh summarizes by saying, "The experience is an instantaneous sense of seeing into the heart of things, as though a universe beyond the universe opened itself wide for an instant and as instantly slammed its doors shut."[1] In grief, it arrives bearing unexpected comfort, a sensation similar to an embrace. The encounters sneak up, unannounced. Near a hospice bed, beside a casket. Or in a little mountain getaway I like to call the Treehouse.

After my mother's death, I spent a weary couple of months feeling lethargic, disconnected. Both of my parents were gone now. The absence of both people who had provided my grounding seemed paramount, and in their place was the vacuous air. Then one autumn day my husband and I took a drive to the Laurel Highlands, because now with my parents gone, I felt drawn to my Western Pennsylvania roots. Perhaps someday, with the generous gift they left me, we would buy a modest weekend getaway; not now, of course. Now it might simply be good to breathe in the freshness and explore.

But then we stepped through the front door of a cozy townhouse and immediately, our eyes were drawn toward the rear windows, situated two stories above ground. A clearing scooped out of the Forbes State Forest treetops revealed glorious mountains beyond, a jewelry box of colors crisscrossing against a clear blue sky. In unison, the exact same words fell from Randy's lips and mine: "Look at that view!" At times, we become so wrapped in our own lives, numbed by exhaustion, that we don't notice God is right there with us, clearing His throat.

When we are embraced by grace, our view is sharpened, so that the presence of God becomes so real and so powerful and so palpable that even amidst loss or disappointment or grief, we are able to feel hope. We are lifted for a moment from sorrow's darkness to partake in a breathtaking view of His overwhelming love. This is the hope that captivates me. The hope that fills the heart with elation. A hope that barely makes sense showing up as it does during this unlikeliest of times. A hope that, to me, can be explained only through the presence of God.

Two moments of grace, though they may appear to be similar, are never exactly the same. They may both inspire awe, considering the element of surprise and the tenderness of the giver, but we have the distinct sense they are customized specifically for us.

"God speaks in the language you know best," writes Oswald Chambers, "not through your ears, but through your circumstances." And so, one person's moment of grace will differ from another's much as the gifts we receive on Christmas morning have been selected and tagged especially for us. At least one element of the gift reflects a cherished experience or a need known only to us and to the giver. The more intensely we experience the moment or the more these gifts pile up, the more seriously we question the notion of mere coincidence.

I think of a book that, through a series of circumstances, landed on a table in the room where my father spent his final days. The book was Norman Vincent Peale's *The Power of Positive Thinking* from which Dad had read to me when I was a child. He would nab me as I tried to sneak past the living room chair where he sat reading Dr. Peale's column in the *Sunday Roto* magazine, and I would end up captive to his and Dad's assertion of how I could accomplish anything to which my mind was set. I stood squirming, impatient as Dad read aloud, underscoring the importance of believing in myself.

It wasn't until adulthood that I would come to appreciate how Dad had nurtured our entire family with his encouraging attitude. The spirit of Dr. Peale's book—and even more, Dad's insistence on living out its principles—was one of the treasured gifts Dad gave me. I knew it. And God knew it. Now decades later with *The Power of Positive Thinking* placed so gently, so lovingly in my hands, I would read to my father, in his dying moments, from the very book he had used to help guide *me*. A gift so perfect, it still leaves me speechless with gratitude.

When we receive a perfect gift during our time of sorrow, we can recognize God as the gift-giver. "Every good and perfect gift is from above, coming down from the Father of heavenly lights, who does not change like shifting shadows,"[2] according to the New Testament's Book of James. And therein lies the similarity among our collective moments of grace. Each and every one, no matter how unique the packaging and presentation, is a reminder of God's unwavering love.

This is not to suggest that we seek the spectacular or scour our grief for a mountaintop incident. John Claypool, a southern pastor who lost his eight-year-old daughter to leukemia, affirmed, "There are moments in the depths of suffering when the soaring of ecstasy would be out of touch with reality, and if this is one's only form of expectation—the only shape of God's strength one can acknowledge—one is sure to feel betrayed and forsaken in the darkness."[3]

Often we experience God's love in the very strength granted to get us through, according to Claypool. With time, in remembrance, the magnitude of the gift is revealed.

"I was given the gift of patience, the gift of enduring," he said. "I was given the strength to 'walk and not faint.'[4] The least of gifts, you say? Maybe so, from one standpoint, yet in another way, it was the most appropriate of all gifts, the one thing most needful in that situation."[5]

There is no denying our deepest hurts. Loss can be brutal. The truth is that this project—this book—was stalled and stalled again as I tried to process the heartache and evil in the world around me. How could I write of hope not only in the face of loss but in spite of a world filled with inexplicable evil?

One evening, a newspaper article told of a homeless man murdered at random by a teenager. A photo showed the teen, his head shaved and wearing an earring, a kid who could have walked down your street or mine. Another showed his victim—middle-aged, bearded, salt-and-pepper hair, kind eyes. According to the article, teen murders of the homeless are on the rise—random acts of violence against those already suffering.

And then on *Oprah*. One day, in the car wash waiting room, I strained to hear the television high in the corner, as my Volkswagen's interior was vacuumed and sprayed in the adjacent garage. Oprah was interviewing a middle-aged man who had been abducted as a thirteen-year-old upon exiting the school bus. For eighteen months, he was held captive, raped and abused before his eventual rescue. His captor was never prosecuted, having been incarcerated for another crime at the time—from which he had since been released—and not wanting to further traumatize the young victim by involving him in a court case, officials never sought to resolve it. Amidst the clanging of metal and sloshing of water, it was difficult to hear the man's voice quietly recounting his ordeal. But everything you needed to know was in his eyes. Overwhelming sadness. A whole life lost.

Why, God, why? I wish I knew.

Explanations abound, humans striving to read God's mind. *God grants us the freedom to make our own choices* is one. But as someone once challenged, knowing the danger and evils in the world, what parent would allow a bunch of three-year-olds to play out in traffic just for the sake of granting independence? *God allows evil for the sake of building character is another.* This explains the atrocities committed against mere children?

I do not know the answer, but I do know this. There are forces of evil in the world. They intend to hurt and destroy and take away that which God has given us. They aim to turn our faith inside out. Look at the schoolhouse shootings of ten young Amish girls here in Lancaster

County where I live. A deranged man drove his pick-up truck up the schoolhouse's gravel drive, walked inside and drew a gun. He dismissed the teacher and other adults, all the boys, and then he lined up the girls, ages six to thirteen, execution-style, and started shooting. Before police broke into the building, he turned the gun and killed himself. Senseless. Terrifying.

How did the victims' families respond? Certainly with deep remorse. Mourning, of course. Grieving. And then with something incredibly surprising: forgiveness. They reached out to the killer's family with kindness and generosity, welcoming them into their homes and their hearts, because they understand that faith means looking away from ourselves and looking to God. Through their example, our Amish neighbors shined a light toward God. Their strength was undeniable. Through them, we felt the warmth of God's love. Even in the face of their darkest nightmare, it was as if they collectively reached up to pull a corner of heaven down to earth, so the rest of us might have a glimpse.

Loss knows no boundaries. It appears on our doorsteps all gussied up in the cruelest of fashions. A person we cherish dies. Someone we love falls terminally ill. Another is snatched away by dementia. "The presence of that absence is everywhere," said Edna St. Vincent Millay. Amazingly, it is precisely through these experiences that our hearts may feel buoyed by the loving embrace of grace.

Psychologist and former pastor Robert H. Justice referred to the 23rd Psalm, a scripture often read at funeral services, in preaching about a string of tragedies occurring in Lancaster County, a bucolic setting but, like anyplace else, harboring a heart full of hurts. In his sermon, Dr. Justice pointed to the psalmist's words *You are with me.*

"We do not have to look away from human suffering and from death," he suggested. "Rather, in the midst of it all we are invited to whisper, *You are with me.* In spite of all the appearances, in the face of heart-breaking diagnosis, in the face of insurmountable pain, even standing at the grave, we are given the words *You are with me.*"

And God *is* with us. The reminders may be subtle. The reprieves from sorrow brief. But as we enter and abide in grief— *integrating pain into life in order to ease the sting*[6]—we can remember, if we choose, that God is with us.

In our everyday lives, even amidst hardship, we encounter patches of heaven right here on earth. We can embrace the hope and belief that the very things Jesus stood for—love, justice, forgiveness and kindness—will win out in the end. We can keep our hearts open and expectant to meet God *now* in ordinary moments. At the sickbed of a loved one. In a crowded arena. Or looking out the window at mountain peaks pointing skyward as if acknowledging the source of their majesty.

In the coming chapters of this book, we will explore various ways that those facing the profound absence of a loved one have described the embrace of grace. The interpretation of these gifts, I should note, is based on my own view of faith; some contributors would agree, while others may not. Many shared their stories in response to an email solicitation I sent to personal acquaintances and business colleagues. Through forwarding, my request also made its way to acquaintances of acquaintances. In no case did I attempt to determine faith commitment, religious affiliation or lack thereof.

In my email, I suggested that whether we have accompanied someone through terminal illness or dementia, or lost them suddenly to death, grief, as author Toby Talbot describes, "comes in unexpected surges. As when nursing, and anything can trigger the onrush of milk. An infant in a carriage or a child crying, but also a traffic light changing, water running, a dog barking. Grief comes out of cups and saucers, empty platforms, hooting whistles, a foghorn blowing, sparrows chirping, sirens screeching, a piano playing, a fern unfurling on my window, tender white mushrooms leaning against one another in their box.

Little alarms these are, transmitted to that network of nerves, muscle, hormone, tissue, and cells that constitute the physical self. Mysterious cues that set off a reminder of grief. It comes crashing like a wave, sweeping me in its crest, twisting me inside out. Then recedes, leaving me broken."[7]

If we are grief-stricken, we know these surges well. We live them day after day. Thankfully, blessedly, there is another side of grief, too. For in the darkness, many of us have been touched by illuminating moments, an upward motion that is equally unexpected. Perhaps a dementia patient makes a profound remark from the place of disconnect. Or a breathtaking view of nature fills us with reprieve. Or a sentiment is expressed that we will remember for the rest of our lives. Or at the bedside, the hospital, the funeral, something uncanny takes us by surprise.

There are endless ways we might be lifted from our deepest sorrow to feel the warmth and power of love. It is in these moments, I believe, that we are blessed with the gift of hope. And it was these moments that I asked the recipients of my email to share.

On the very same day that I sent the email, replies started appearing in my in-box. They came from men and women, ages twenty-seven to eighty, representing a variety of backgrounds, from medical professionals to educators to clergy to corporate executives and artists. The generous outpouring of stories from men and women who had graciously accepted the divine amidst the darkness was inspiring and affirmed the patterns of grace I had come to experience in my own times of loss. Though each was unique, common *varieties* of these gifts surfaced from the stories to help define the shape of this book.

For example, some of us find healing through memories of the deceased: the unruliness of his eyebrows, the way her pink chiffon nightgown twirled around her like cotton candy, as she pirouetted giggling. Or we encounter some of life's most valuable lessons: what compassion looks like, how we might more purposefully allocate our time. Or we gratefully accept the gift of art—music, drawing, writing—to soothe us through the sadness. This is just to name a few.

The array of gifts is impressive, and in the pages to come, we will explore many of them. This is not an effort to establish a mall directory of the stores in which God goes gift shopping. No, the beauty of these gifts is their uniqueness, a perfection that could only be crafted by the one who loves each and every one of us the best. What our common encounters do offer is a revelation not only that God blesses us individually but that by sharing our graces with each other, we extend God's love, thus embracing one another through our collective sorrows.

When my older daughter went away to college, the heartache of loss pierced through me. I remember standing at the doorway of her empty bedroom where the vacuum cleaner's streaks on her carpet were so pronounced in their tidiness that I stomped right through them. The house felt barren without her.

Then my friend Eleanor told me of the day she'd taken her son away to college. Upon her return home, she discovered Alan's napkin still at the breakfast table where he'd left it that morning. Eleanor sat down at the table, picked up his napkin and wept into it. The comfort I received from knowing my friend had muddled her way through my exact same heartache was encouraging. I knew that she understood. And that she had made it through.

So also it is with hope. When we share our glimmers of hope, we lift each other up. We affirm one another's longing to believe.

There is a saying that goes, "A candle loses nothing by lighting another candle." If you are caring for a person who is dying, or grieving the loss of someone you loved, hold out your candle. There are many who wish to light it or to light theirs from yours. For if there is one thing I have learned along this treacherous path called loss, it is that none of us travels alone.

For Writing & Reflection
Think about a moment in which you were lifted from the darkness of sorrow. Describe what happened. What did that moment feel like?

"In search of

my mother's garden,

I found my own."

Alice Walker

two
embraced by
discovery

meeting
anew

As we accompany the dying on their journey, or even after they are gone, certain truths about their character and the relationships we shared with them may come to light. For better or worse, some traits will be all too familiar, while others may take us by surprise. The very fact that we are experiencing another person in hugely altered circumstances —in the shadows of loss   affects our view. Somewhere along the spectrum of time—in the final days of life or weeks, months, even years after the death—we are likely to see anew that which we've taken for granted or that which has gone unnoticed. It can be a gift to encounter a glimpse of the dying or the deceased through new eyes—through God's eyes—for if we decide to embrace this enlightened perspective, we may enjoy enriched relationships, meaningful exchanges or the will to forgive or receive forgiveness, endeavors that unveil God's healing grace.

The evening our mother died in a hospice bed, my sister Pat was at her side. It had been a challenging six years since, newly widowed, she had moved north from Florida to live in the same town as Pat and me and our families. As her dementia worsened, the fears, anxieties and distrustful nature that had dominated her life intensified. My sister and I struggled to exercise patience and compassion—we prayed for these things—as Mother deteriorated, underscoring the distance we had felt from her for much of our lives. Finally, a fall and fractured hip landed Mother in the hospital where she suffered respiratory failure and was transferred to a bed at the Essa Flory Hospice Center.

> ## I had never encountered this person before.
> **—Pat**

In her final moments, Pat stood next to her, holding her hand.

"I told her that God loved her and that He was waiting for her," Pat remembers. "She simply stared at me, her eyes wide and filled with trust. I had never encountered this person before. It seemed that all of her inhibitions and fears had vanished. She was at peace and close to God. She then slept, and shortly thereafter, she took her last breath. I felt God's presence in the room."

If we let it, God's presence brings with it a sense of calm, perhaps a shift in the spirit of the dying or in the way we experience them. As we accompany others on their final journey, whether our relationship with them was ideal or something less than that, seeking and recognizing God's presence leads to peace. For in that endeavor, we are no longer focused on our frustrations, our disappointments or the shortcomings of the relationship; the embrace of God's grace trumps all of them.

Discovering God's plan, I have learned, often requires a redirection of our own expectations. It may seem that one door after another is closing before us, dashing any chance of fulfilling the hopes we'd had for the relationship. We can start "pounding on the door that just closed," as author Parker Palmer describes. Or, we can turn around and trust God to reveal another way.[8]

In our case, Mother's journey into dementia triggered mourning for what might have been but never was, a door slamming on the unrealized parts of a relationship that we had craved. But in the end, we realized that God was there for us. We were able to see Mother as a blessed child of God, journeying through life's storms back to His arms. This insight has been an amazing act of grace.

A new sense of relationship comes upon us in various ways, a testament to God's endless creativity in inviting us to arrive at our own surprise party. As different as the invitation may be for each of us, once accepted, the gift is clearly a newfound ability to see through love-filled eyes.

For Pat, a glimpse of trust on Mother's face moved my sister's heart. For me, as I mentioned earlier, the invitation came via Mother's aura of contentment as she lay in her casket. Her genuine smile, illuminated by God's love, relieved me of the burden I had erroneously assumed as mine all those years: the responsibility for Mother's happiness. The grace I received was the elucidation that God, *not I*, was, always had been, and always would be, Mother's caretaker.

For my friend Francie and her siblings, the invitation arrived in the final hours of the life of their father, a recent widower. It was delivered by a stream of employees parading into his room at Barclay Friends, the retirement community he'd called home for five years. A victim of Parkinson's disease, now complicated by a hip fracture from having fallen out of his wheelchair, Francie's ninety-one-year-old father was winding down, his mottled hands, cold feet, shallow and erratic breathing all signs of imminent death.

On a Saturday afternoon, Francie and two of her four siblings gathered at their father's bed, praying that another sister's flight from Colorado would arrive in time.

"It had been a fairly complicated relationship for all of us," Francie, the youngest of the siblings, explains. Though her dad had been a kind and loving father, a man of deep integrity who was highly successful in business and civic work, there came a time, as kids left home, that "things got tricky."

Her father, she says, "in a presidential appointee position in Washington, D.C., was devastated when Nixon resigned, eighteen months later his job was taken, and he found himself retired not by his choosing. And then he began to drink heavily." A difficult couple of decades followed for this man, for their mother and for all of them, including when they brought grandchildren to visit.

"It was just very hard," recalls Francie, "and Mom, convinced that alcoholism was not a disease but a measure of self-discipline, was not able to help him. None of us were."

Now, as they awaited their sister Meg's arrival, "there started a trickle of caregivers from the building...they had heard that Dad was failing, and they came to say good-bye." Before long, the three siblings were witnessing an onset of tender good-byes, so many in fact, that Francie muses it was as if there were a sign-up sheet or a line forming in the hallway.

"They just kept stopping by…people who had helped Dad in physical therapy, the activities director, laundress, nurse after aide after maintenance person." As they bid her father good-bye, Francie was struck by the emotion and love in the eyes of all those who had cared for and cared about her father in the previous five years.

Then each of them, she recalls, would "turn to us and tell us what they had experienced of Dad—what they knew, what they lived, what they loved about him."

"He always asked about my kids."

"He has the most beautiful blue eyes."

"He loved to talk about his family."

"Even now he is still so handsome."

"He was always so polite."

"He was always so positive, even on the really hard days."

"He loved you all so much."

"He always enjoyed his food—especially his chocolates."

"He never lost his sparkle."

"He was such a man of integrity."

"He found so much pleasure in the little things—especially his chocolates."

"He was so proud of his children and grandchildren."

"He always tried so hard to cooperate when we were trying to help him."

"He loved a good joke."

"He loved his birds."

"He loved to laugh."

"He loved to tell us who was who in the family photo."

And on and on and on.

"As my sister Buff, my brother Bob and I sat there and watched this all transpire over the course of about two hours, we became acutely aware that something was happening before our very eyes and to our very eyes," Francie recalls. "We each had our issues with our relationship with Dad. We had gone over and over it in the course of the previous three days since Bob had come to town. Expectations, silences, seeming detachment, distance in the relationship, complications of Mom's strong personality and Dad's desire to be affirmed…it was complicated for each of us in our own different ways…

"And then the Barclay Friends Employee Parade. One by one they showed us a snapshot. They had not known Mom. They had not known Dad. They just knew the man they had worked with during the previous five years, and they showed us who they had come to love.

"By hour #2, we were overwhelmed with an awareness of God in all that was happening. God in each care-giver, God in Dad, God in the room. He was…gently…showing us our dad as He saw him, as He created him.

> "
> Life had muddied the picture for us, Dad's offspring, but God in His supreme graciousness was showing us the clear picture before Dad died.
>
> **—Francie**
>
> "

Life had muddied the picture for us, Dad's offspring, but God in His supreme graciousness was showing us the clear picture before Dad died. It was overwhelming…

"And when the parade subsided, we talked together and we talked to Dad. We asked him to forgive us and we told him we forgave him, and we cried and hugged and hung onto our dad until, if he had been lucid, he would have told us, 'Enough already!'"

After their sister Meg arrived, their father rallied, his hands and feet turning warm and pink, alive to his children with the qualities with which God had blessed him. The siblings had another day-and-a-half with their father before he died, every precious minute of it able to view him in a new light. They marveled over this gift, then marveled again that each, individually, had been reminded of verse 12 from 1 Corinthians 13 affirming their glimpse of heaven: "Now we see but a poor reflection as in a mirror; then we shall see face to face. Now I know in part; then I shall know fully, even as I am fully known."

This grace—the ability to remove our own smudged glasses to take in the merciful view of God—may also appear after the loss occurs. In fact, the advantages of space and time can help clarify perspective. Author Patrice Gaines explains it this way.

"The gift—the grace—from my mother's death, and maybe from any death, is that we begin to ponder the life of the deceased in a way we do not and cannot while the person is alive…Pondering my mother's life has been a wondrous, enriching experience for me.

"When my mother was alive, my appreciation of her was hindered by my relationship to her—by our disagreements, our own selfishness, our busy schedules. We had a great relationship, but what stopped it from being perfect was life itself, the roles we had chosen and been born into. After her death, I invested hours in poring over every minute of her life I could recall. I would not have spent my time that way had she still been alive.

> ❝
>
> ...when I think about my mother, what I remember is mostly the good. The easiest things for me to forget were the same things that kept us apart when she was alive.
>
> **—Patrice Gaines**
>
> ❞

"Did my moment of grace explain her death, or relieve my pain? No. But it changed my feelings about my mother. I know that when I think about my mother, what I remember is mostly the good. The easiest things for me to forget were the same things that kept us apart when she was alive."[9]

Some of us may gain clarified perspectives within months of the loss; for others, especially in cases where the relationship was complex, it may take years. This is not to say that unresolved issues will suddenly right themselves or miraculously eradicate feelings of guilt or anger. But over time, with hearts open to God, forgiveness may turn out to be the healing grace.

After years of harboring anger and confusion toward a mother who had committed suicide, therapist and author David Treadway eventually composed a letter to her as part of a twenty-six-year endeavor to sort out his feelings.

"For years I felt that I had forgiven you for murdering yourself. That was bullshit," Treadway wrote in his letter. "Beneath the smoothly polished facade of forgiveness, I was dead inside. I hated you and I hated me for hating you. And I felt nothing at all.

"It's been twenty-six years now. For most of that time, I never gave you a second thought. Now, I can't get you out of my mind. This is progress?

"Mom, I think it's time to really forgive you, and maybe even me. But I'm still mad. I just don't know how to let go of it. Believe it or not, I've been trying to pray about it. I've also begun to write it all down. It's a form of prayer, too.

"But I don't really know what I'm doing. I'm just here.

"I've never said thank you, Mom. I've never really acknowledged how much love and joy you gave all of us. How much the best part of me comes from the best part of you. I am proud to have been in your parade."[10]

Forgiveness can be an immense undertaking. It is a supreme act of love. Entire books have been written on the subject. Perhaps there is no example more powerful than the fact that Jesus Christ died to forgive. And what richness in the message that the forgiver finds new life!

A colleague of mine recalls reading a book years ago

that included a chapter on the power of forgiveness. In it, an exercise encouraged the reader to write down the name of someone he or she needed to forgive and to specify what had been done that needed forgiving. Various steps walked the participant through the process.

"There had been some long-term tension with my father going back to the '70s and the clash between my becoming more free and independent, and his attempts to assert what he thought was legitimate parental authority in defense of values he held," Steve recalls. "I was mostly compliant, but harbored resentment and cut off most real communication between us.

"Well, I went through the process and confronted my own resentment and unforgiveness of him. I never said anything to him, but when he was hospitalized a couple of weeks later I found that it was much easier to visit him and talk to him. So that alone would have been grace. But when he unexpectedly died during that hospitalization, I was extremely thankful to have been given the opportunity to go through that process and experience a little bit of a change in our relationship."

Like coming to terms with our expectations in deference to God's plan, forgiveness also requires a redirection of plans. God nudges us to relinquish control. When we do, we discover a divine agenda that carries us through in a way that we could have never mustered on our own.

The Reverend Randolph T. Riggs, in a sermon entitled "Words about Love in Human Conduct," suggested that "perhaps we need to understand the behavior which we deplore having its roots in the unmet need of the person who would do us harm." This is God's view. Call it compassion or perceptiveness; it does not mean that we must accept or embrace the errant behavior. It simply helps us to see it for what it is and where it came from, to remove the burden from our own hearts and to move on with life unfettered by the past.

As deep as is the yearning for a long-awaited apology, the first step toward resolution may need to be taken by the injured party. Though it is not impossible, expecting a shift in the behavior of the dying may be unrealistic.

"People die as they live—intensified," wrote hospice nurse and author Maggie Callanan. "Nice people get nicer. Busy people get busier, even if only in their dreams. Quiet people get quieter. Demanding people demand more. Manipulators will surpass their past controlling behavior."[11]

We may need to turn away from the door that has been shut before us, the door behind which we believed we would find the acknowledgement of wrongdoing or the apology. By letting God show us another way, as my colleague Steve did, we can still be comforted with a peaceful resolution.

Letting go of qualities that were less than endearing is a lovely gift that God offers in our sorrow. Conversely, qualities that we *cherished* in the dying offer a welcome familiarity as we navigate the foreign territory of grief. Embracing them as gifts can be a source of peace.

I think of my father greeting the hospice nurse upon opening his eyes from an afternoon nap. When she asked how his day was going, he smiled and replied, "Better, now that you're here." Of course. This was the same big-hearted man who used to show up in our driveway with a car full of children from Pittsburgh's St. Christopher's Orphanage, welcoming them to our home to share the holidays with us.

And my sister Lena, never wanting to inconvenience others, even as she succumbed to cancer. How true to her considerate nature, we marveled, that her time of death coordinated with the holiday visit the rest of us had already planned to our hometown of Pittsburgh, as though she were sparing us the inconvenience of circling back again on the Pennsylvania Turnpike for the funeral.

And my friend Elaine, struggling with terminal illness, yet ever efficient and organized. In all her Elaine-ness, she took her sixteen-year-old shopping for prom dresses and—just in case—bought three of them on sale, knowing she wouldn't be around to help her daughter shop for them when the time came.

This juxtaposition of loss and gratitude for those we are losing is bittersweet, an example of God tempering grief with familiar endearments.

An acquaintance of mine recalls facing a four-and-a-half-hour drive to Western Pennsylvania after her father, a leukemia patient, suffered a massive cerebral hemorrhage. Deb rushed to get her children from school, gather some clothes from home and, after her husband arrived from work, start the trip.

Halfway there, her sister called to share the doctors' belief that the only way her father would live long enough for Deb to see him was to intubate him. Apologetically, her sister asserted that she didn't want to do that to him, and Deb agreed, "He should go when God feels it's time to go." Her sister told their father that Deb was on her way, to try to hold on.

"That was exactly what he did," Deb recalls. "Within fifteen minutes of my entering the room and telling him I was there, my father began to fail. His pulse rate dropped. The nurses remarked how he had waited until I arrived. I sat on his bed, stroked his arm and told him how much

I loved him. His eyes were closed, and there was no physical response to my touch, but I could see tears in the outside corner of his eye. Within one hour of my entering the room, my father was dead.

"He fought so hard to give me the opportunity to say good-bye," Deb writes. "My father was a selfless, generous man his whole life, and he showed that until the very end."

And so God is there. Nudging us to see what we'd already seen but now, in His light, even more magnificently. Or helping us to see differently—through God's eyes and with God's brand of love. In these ways, it is as if we are meeting the dying anew. A gift so generous, so welcome amidst heartbreaking sorrow, it can only be viewed as grace.

For Writing & Reflection

Write a letter to someone you are losing or have lost. Describe the qualities you cherished in your relationship. Express any hurt you may have felt from his or her behavior. If you try to understand that behavior as being rooted in unmet needs, how does this alter your hurt?

"Healing from grief is not

the process of forgetting. It is the

process of remembering with

less pain and more joy."

Author Unknown

three
embraced by
memories

empowering the
present

Memories rejuvenate connections with those we have loved and lost. For some, the time will be right to entertain the notion of memories as gifts. For others, the sting of loss may seem to be at odds with the joy of remembering. Author Gerald L. Sittser, who experienced catastrophic loss when his wife, his mother and his four-year-old daughter were instantly killed in a car accident, described the ambivalence in recalling the details of their life together.

"I cannot live with the memories," he wrote, "and I cannot live without them."[12]

For those who grieve, the essential element we must allow ourselves— however brief or vast we require it to be—is time. If we feel ready and when we feel ready, remembering the past, as someone once said, gives power to the present.

Memories may take us by surprise like trick candles

on a birthday cake suddenly reigniting. Or they can purposefully be summoned for paying tribute, recapturing the
essence of those whose loss we mourn. These gestures, no
matter how simple, provoke a sense of inner peace. Many
choose to resurrect them in celebration of their loved
one's life.

And so my friend Jeanne placed her mother's favorite
crocheted afghan over her casket as it was wheeled into
church for the funeral mass.

My friends Mike and Brie handed four red helium-
filled balloons to their two-year-old son, Cole, to release
at the grave of his infant brother, commemorating Luke's
four short hours of life.

Another sprinkled her father's ashes across the finish
line at the Atlantic City Racetrack where he spent many
Saturday nights.

"That's what he wanted," Pam explains. "I often wonder if the horses who ran that night felt his spirit there,
cheering them on as they thundered across the finish line.
I know I still do."

"These memories form an interior altar, a place of
connection to the dead," writes author Nancy Cobb.
"Remembering is an act of resurrection, each repetition
a vital layer of mourning, in memory of those we are sure
to meet again."[13]

My friend Zenta's father lived the kind of life that inspired others even after he was gone. Some called him "big Al." Others lovingly referred to him as "Alfred the Great." So it was no surprise that scores of those whose lives he had touched made the trek to a New Jersey shore town to celebrate the life of this highly regarded former professor, author and expert in the world of strength training for sports, longevity and overall health. In Al's memory, his family dedicated an engraved bench on the boardwalk overlooking the beach that he loved. After the service and luncheon at a nearby hotel, family and friends set out for a walk to "Al's bench."

"Since he was cremated," Zenta shares, "the bench gives my mother and all of us a place to go to 'be with' Dad. She walks there every day. It's incredibly healing." About thirty guests stayed overnight, and the next morning, they met for breakfast.

"The group of us decided to meet again next May Day weekend for another honorary walk," Zenta writes. "The 2nd Annual 'Alfred the Great' Promenade and Pancake Breakfast."

And so for Zenta, her family and friends, a ritual was established: an event to gather them together to pay homage to a man whose life had enriched their own lives. Other occasions encourage remembrances, as well: a loved one's birthday, for example, Mother's Day, Father's Day, shared holidays, even the date of death or burial. At first, we may feel overcome with loss as the special day arrives. Letting ourselves feel the sadness as we receive God's embrace helps to nourish the soul.

Author Patrice Gaines remembers the hesitation she initially felt the first time her late mother's birthday approached.

"As the months after her death rolled by and her birthday neared, the first birthday we would celebrate without her," Gaines writes, "I felt anxiety building in my heart. How would I be able to live through the day? How would I mourn? What should I do? When I woke up that morning, the answer seemed so clear: as I made up my bed, I began to sing. 'Happy birthday to you! Happy birthday to you! Happy birthday, dear Mamma! Happy birthday to you!' I sang louder and louder and I applauded for a long time, cheering my mother, giving thanks to God for allowing her to be my mother, showing my appreciation for the life she had lived and the joy she had left behind."[14]

In my family, birthdays and the date of death—of my parents, of two sisters—usually elicit an acknowledgment among my surviving sisters and me. "This is the day that Daddy died," one of us will mention. Or, "Today would have been Dee's birthday." For me, it helps to know that others, even after many years have passed, miss them as I do.

Recently I spent several days alone in the mountains, making the transition from the hectic pace of summer to the more predictable routine of fall. There are many reasons I love the mountains; among them is the fact that my father was drawn to this setting, cultivating an appreciation for nature in me, as well. Dad could spot a deer from miles away, and when he did, his uncontainable sense of awe vitalized everyone around him.

Because part of the relaxation of this kind of retreat is not knowing or caring about the date, or even about the time of day for that matter, I was not thinking about the fact that the anniversary of my father's death, September 6th, fell on one of the five days of my getaway. But on that very day, I was hiking along a mountain road when a rustle in the woods caught my attention.

Suddenly less than twenty feet away, two magnificent deer appeared from the brush and crossed the path in front of me. I stopped in my tracks, stunned. Then another deer came out of the woods, paused to look at me, and continued across the road. Just as I was wishing for my camera, there was more rustling of leaves, and three more deer pranced across the path in front of me. It was breathtaking.

As I continued my walk, my heart was fluttering

with excitement, and of course, the memory of my father came alive. The sound of his overjoyed voice. His animated description of the six deer—how many antlers each sported, the flicker of the third deer's eyelids—a story he'd repeat to everyone he happened upon…the grocery store clerk, the bank teller, a neighbor raking the lawn. The memory was so vivid, it was as if Dad were right there with me. And in that moment of reliving a walk side by side with him—similar to the way, when I was a child, we had hiked through the Alleghenies—God showed me a glimpse of a heavenly reunion with Dad. I was filled with hope.

As if this reminder weren't gift enough, soon after returning home, I realized that my encounter with the six deer (on the *sixth* of September, no less) occurred on the very date of my father's passing. It has been eight years, and I still miss him very much. The miracle to me is how God continues to embrace me in my sorrow, even after all this time and even when that sorrow is not prominent in my awareness.

Pastor and author Sam Oliver aptly refers to these gifts of remembrance as "holy moments of recollection." When we experience them, the spirit of the person we have lost comes back in a way that hints of a sacred reunion.

Some survivors choose to pay tribute with remembrances that touch the lives of others, as well. A handful write books, such as Mitch Albom's *Tuesdays with Morrie*, or Joan Didion's *The Year of Magical Thinking* or Madeleine L'Engle's *The Summer of the Great-Grandmother*, to name just a few. Others become involved in volunteering for a cause to which their loved one was committed, as Patrice Gaines contemplated upon the remembrance of her mother's birthday.

"On my mother's birthdays henceforth," she writes, "I decided to dedicate the day…to doing some good in her name. Perhaps I will volunteer to feed the homeless, a service my mother did in the latter part of her life, or maybe I will talk to young women about how to change their lives. I just know that I want to show my joy on that day—not my sorrow. I want to say: 'Your death has reminded me of the importance of love and your life was an example of that.' I want to give thanks."[15]

Author Christopher Noël, a former writing teacher of mine, created Tall Rock Retreat, a writers' retreat in Calais, Vermont, inspired in part by the life and work of his father, who passed away suddenly. Here writers go to seek solitude, staying in small cabins away from the clutter of everyday life to work on their writing.

"My father held great reverence for *place*," Chris notes on the Tall Rock web site. A Jung scholar whose career included writing on the nature of the imagination and of language, Chris's father traveled to the British Isles in search of ancient sites, "sacred spaces" often built in stone, experiences that Chris often shared with him. Now at the entrance to the secluded property, rich in natural beauty, Chris had a 17-ton, 28-foot-long piece of granite erected in honor of his father, after scattering several handfuls of his father's ashes in the deep hole dug to accommodate the monolith.[16]

> " My father held great reverence for place.
> —Chris "

Similar to Chris's effort to perpetuate his father's life passion, my former colleague Brian, joined by family and friends, took on a major project to pay tribute after the sudden death of his son.

"Jeffrey loved baseball," his father writes. "He played pitcher and first base. He lived for the big strikeout. He loved to put on his uniform and run out to the mound to start a game."

When Jeffrey was ten years old, complications of an aggressive blood clot in his head ended his short life.

"Jeff sought out fun so enthusiastically and so successfully," his father observes, "that it was almost as if he knew he had to hurry."

As they navigated the path of heart-wrenching grief, Jeff's family, in conjunction with a nearby church, began raising funds for the building of a new baseball field "where kids will be excited to play and learn the game." The field is known as "Jeffy's Field."

"The outpouring of support so far has been over-whelming," notes a message on www.jeffysfield.com, a web site developed to support the effort.

"We miss Jeff every minute of every day," according to a letter from his family, including mom, dad, older sister and younger brother, "but we are comforted in knowing how many people still celebrate his life and remember what a great kid he was."

In addition to raising money for the field, the family has also set up a fund for making annual donations to local organizations that further the cause of youth baseball and instruction. One fundraiser, a silent auction, raised nearly $20,000, most of which was earmarked for distribution through the fund.

"This is all just a natural response, I think, to this un-natural order of life," writes Brian. "Parents who lose kids often find it hard to stop caring for them, so they find other ways."

Whether it is a writers' retreat in Vermont or a baseball

> ❝
> He loved to put on his uniform and run out to the mound to start a game.
> —Brian
> ❞

field in Maryland, the act of building inspires hope. Hope that the life of the deceased will touch the lives of others. Hope that one person's passions will live on in others who are somehow encouraged to carry on similar dreams.

Remembering the life of a loved one in simpler forms is no less significant.

For some, memory ignites itself upon the discovery of mementoes left behind. We re-visit photos, listen to a voice recording or pore over old letters. In doing so, we may find ourselves yearning for the person we've lost at the same time that the spirit of ever-presence embraces us.

My colleague Betsy lost her father long before he died. She remembers, as a young child, dancing on his feet and riding on his back as he crawled on his hands and knees. Her early life in Pelham, New York, seemed idyllic, complete with honeysuckle lining the long drive to the family's home.

Suddenly one day, "oblivious to the horrible storm brewing" in their house, young Betsy found herself leaving "on a vacation" with her mother and two sisters who

were much older than she. It turned out that the four of
them stayed in Sun Valley a whole month, the time during
which her parents' divorce was being finalized back
home. Betsy never got an explanation or answers to her
questions.

"There was hardly a night that went by that I wasn't
weeping," she remembers, "because I missed him so much."

Like Nancy Drew in the novels to which she escaped,
Betsy, at age nine, became a sleuth. Because her questions
about her missing father continued to go unanswered, she
also became "very prayerful," she says, hoping she would
find a clue Nancy Drew-style, perhaps a hidden note. Her
prayer was answered when she came upon a photograph
in the attic of her family's home.

In the photo, her father's "legs are stretched over the
sofa," she explains. "The newspaper is over his ankles and
he's holding me as an infant and looking down." Excited
and curious, young Betsy carefully pulled the small pho
tograph out of its frame.

"There was a cardboard stand in back," she says. "In
between the cardboard and the photo was his calling card.
On the back of the calling card in his handwriting was a
note that said, 'Daddy loves Betsy.'"

When Betsy turned twenty-one, upon learning from
her grandmother that her father was living in Brooklyn,

she was determined to visit him. One month later, before Betsy was able to make the trip, he died.

"Once every two years I totally break down and weep over my father," she admits. Her grief is undeniable. The photo and her father's note may seem like tiny mementoes of the loving man she barely remembers, and they certainly cannot replace the enormous love lost. But when she called me to schedule a time to discuss her experience, she said, "I'd like to share a treasure with you."

A treasure! This was her description of the photo she discovered in which she is being held by the father she loved and lost, accompanied by the love note tucked inside. It is a perfect metaphor for the way God embraces us in our sorrow and for the words of comfort He whispers in our ears.

These tangible remembrances, as small as they may seem to be, play important roles in healing from grief. A woman named Krissa wrote to me about her mother who passed away from ovarian cancer after a four-year battle. In those four years, Krissa notes, her mother did her best to prepare herself and her family for her final journey. In a folder she'd labeled "Last Things," her mother had saved articles on loss and grief, the funeral plans she'd carefully prepared with the priest, as well as personal letters to those closest to her.

"I knew all the time that my letter was there in the folder waiting for me, and before she passed away, I dreaded reading it," Krissa recalls. "But now, it is precious to me.

"Although what she wrote was not news to me—our love for each other was never in question; we didn't leave any unresolved issues that needed to be put to rest in a letter—it is a gift. I pick up the letter when I'm especially missing her or at times when I would have called her to get some advice. It's a reminder of how special I was to her, her encouragement for the challenges that come in life, and how much she's looking forward to being together again in Heaven.

> " **It's a reminder of how special I was to her.**
> —Krissa

"Reading her letter is certainly not the same as talking to her," adds Krissa, "but seeing her handwriting and hearing her voice through her writing is a comfort each time I pick up my envelope and unfold the pages."

Even in the ordinary course of day-to-day life, we come upon these treasures, and suddenly the connection rekindles. This has happened to me while searching for menu ideas, for example. I'll be turning the plastic pocket pages of my loose-leaf cookbook and there, scribbled in my late sister Dee's handwriting, is a recipe for strawberry Jell-O salad. Or another recipe for carrot cake neatly printed by my late friend Elaine. The simple reminders of their culinary talents have helped me recall the nurturing spirits of these women I loved.

Or I pull open the drawer beneath our living room television set, and there is a DVD of my mother sending greetings to family who were to gather at a reunion she was unable to attend. My daughter and I visited Mother and recorded the video shortly before she fell, broke her hip and died. And now here it is, an endearing image of my feisty ninety-two-year-old mother attempting to convince viewers of her well-being. I am overcome with gratitude realizing that God orchestrated the videotaping—two weeks before Mother died—so that someday, the watching of it would fill me with warmth.

Likewise, the sound of my father's voice on tape recounting his life stories brings back the spirit of vitality that I always treasured in him. I had interviewed Dad years before he died, not long after one of his heart surgeries. Realizing that time might be short, I wanted to capture his story in his own words. My sister Pat recently had the set of cassettes I'd recorded transferred to CD. From this, I received one of the greatest gifts of comfort since Dad's death.

It occurred while I was driving home from one of my trips to the Laurel Highlands. Since I was alone, it was a perfect opportunity to listen once again to Dad's stories. The CDs are stored in the pocket of my car door, so I retrieved one and popped it into my car's player.

After making a brief side trip to Johnstown, I asked a store clerk for directions to the Pennsylvania Turnpike. The route she suggested took me through the rural roads of Windber, which happens to be the city where my father was born. I can barely describe the richness, as I drove through the countryside of my father's birth town, listening to his voice express the joys and sorrows he remembered as a boy growing up there.

How tender God's embrace is! It is unmistakable, the grace that soothes, that understands the emptiness of loss, that somehow fills it with sacred comfort. A memory, a tribute, a remembrance. They are heartfelt gifts on which we discover God's signature, the handwriting full of promise.

Here. I chose this one especially for you. With all my love.

For Writing & Reflection

Write a list of one-hundred memories of someone you've loved and lost. They may be simple or profound: the cowlick in his hair or the day you climbed a mountain together. Just put pen to paper and write anything that comes to mind.

If you are a caregiver, consider interviewing the patient for whom you are caring, asking questions about his or her life. If possible, capture the conversation on tape or digital recorder. The project may take days or weeks to complete, but there are gifts to be discovered in the quality of the time spent together, the affirmation of the patient's life stories and later, the legacy to treasure.

"Laughing together can be a time of intimacy and communion, a time when we come forward, fully present, and touch into each other's humanness and vulnerability."

Barry Sultanhoff, M.D.

four
embraced by
humor

a spoon
on her nose

colleague of mine remembers the grief and tears when his sixteen-year-old niece died in a car accident six months after she got her driver's license. He also recalls his surprise at his family's laughter as they sorted through photos to create a picture board for the funeral.

"We found ourselves remembering a lot of goofy things she said and did," Steve shares, "like balancing a spoon on her nose at a family outing in Hatteras, or the way she would say random phrases to a French exchange student she had become friends with, phrases she had learned in French class but that had absolutely nothing to do with anything happening at the moment.

"That evening going through those pictures and being able to laugh in the midst of incredible sorrow was for me one of the most comforting experiences of those days."

Grief is a time that begs us to be genuine. When we

are moved to cry, we must let the tears flow. They are cleansing, and they trigger healing. So it also is with laughter. Specifically, I speak of loving laughter, the kind of humor that inspires "a time of intimacy and communion," as Sultanhoff describes.

For some, it may seem unthinkable to entertain laughter while in a state of overwhelming sorrow. But isn't God the master of paradox? Don't the leaves display their most awesome colors in the exact same season that they fall? Don't we celebrate the lives of our loved ones at the very time that we mourn their loss?

> 66
> ...being able to laugh in the midst of incredible sorrow was for me one of the most comforting experiences of those days.
> —Steve
> 99

If we were meant to be one-dimensional beings, God would have left us on the drawing board and called it a day. As humans, we are multi-dimensional and our complexities are cause for celebration. God uses them to keep us balanced. The more we look to God as master of our spirit, the more appreciative we become of life's ambiguities.

Writer and editor Joseph Dunn goes so far as to state that "those whose confidence rests in God and not in themselves are free to laugh and play in a way not available to others."

Thus, just as we mourn the grip of dementia on a quick-witted parent, for example, we are treated to an uncanny observation from the place of disconnect. Or the eulogist recalls an amusing incident, rekindling the spirit of the deceased. These are "holy hugs," as one pastor described them, moments to savor God's attentiveness.

"It may take some time to find laughter after a loss," according to author Allen Klein. "It may not always be the fall-down-hold-your-belly kind of laughter...sometimes it's only an inner chuckle. But whatever kind it is, it is there. It is there to provide a momentary respite from our grief. It is there to show us that indeed life goes on in spite of our loss. It is there to give us hope."[17]

When we allow the seeds of humor to sprout, suddenly we are in familiar territory. Humor calls forth a place of comfort, and this connection puts us at ease, as Steve's family found when they recalled his niece's antics. When we are entrenched in the foreign soil of grief, we *need* patches of the familiar. It is no wonder then that God often uses family to deliver them.

The evening after our mother's death, the moonlight softened the darkness as my sisters and I drove along Route 8. It had been a long day. We had made the four-hour drive from Lancaster, where Mother had taken her last breath at a hospice center, to our hometown of Pittsburgh, where she would be buried. We had settled in at the hotel. We had met with the funeral director, choosing the casket, the holy cards, the hymns to be sung at the funeral mass. We had eaten dinner at a nearby restaurant, and now we were searching for another restaurant at which we might gather the rest of our families who were to arrive the following day for the viewing.

In the back seat of Pat's car, reality was starting to settle in.

"Do you realize we're orphans now?" I asked.

Marge, the oldest of the three of us and the perennial teaser, began to laugh. "I wonder if someone will take us in." Her laughter bounced off the windshield.

"I'm tired," I pleaded. "Let's go back to the hotel."

"Why did you pick this orphan, Pat?" Marge pushed. "I don't want this one. Maybe they'll give us a different one."

Pat steered toward the Hulton Bridge.

"Should we check out restaurants in Oakmont?" she suggested.

"No!" I said. "This is too far. I need to go back."

"Why did you pick this orphan?" Marge repeated. "She's a whiny one!"

"I picked her because she sort of looks like me," Pat said.

We all laughed and could not stop. Punchy laughter, tears running down our cheeks. Once Marge got started, there was no turn-off switch. As usual, her teasing was relentless.

"Stop it!" I pleaded. "I have to go to the bathroom!"

Then we laughed even harder, uncontrollably. It had to be God's grace, the granting of respite so deep in our hearts. And how better to receive such a gift than within the safe haven of sisterhood? For those of us so blessed, the lifelong bonds offer comfort. With family, we can be ourselves. We can let loose. When family surrounds us permitting us to laugh and be who we are, tension can be broken and healing kicks in.

Editor and author DeWitt Henry writes of his sister, his brothers and their spouses traveling to Villanova from various parts of the country to their parents' retirement home after their father died. He recalls the events after the burial.

"I remember our returning home and eating, eating, eating ravenously. Halloween was only a day or so away, and perhaps our most genuine gesture, as bizarre and true as we felt we were, was while on some errand, on impulse to go into the local toy store, Halligans—a mecca at least of my own childhood—and buy clear plastic masks, the kind that eerily distort your features into Nixon's, say. We wore them driving back to Villanova, and laughed and laughed together as we tried on different faces for each other, my mother too."[18]

Anyone who has provided long-term care for the terminally ill, even in the best of circumstances, knows what it means to need a respite from the intensity. Day after day, week after week of dealing with the unexpected, navigating the confusing halls of healthcare, trading sleep for the more urgent need to cry: the process takes a toll. In times like these, humor, even in the smallest dose, can be a reminder of God's presence. Amazingly, the patient herself may be the one chosen to deliver this respite.

Henry recalls when his mother, who suffered degenerative heart failure, came close to dying. She "said she thought she had gone over, but she wasn't good enough. They'd thrown her back, like an undersized fish."[19]

Like emissaries from God, these patients draw upon the illness itself, as though handed a vehicle with which to leave the most loving of parting gifts, a lifting of spirits. Not all dying patients maintain this degree of perspective and balance, but when they do, it affirms the qualities we treasure in them. And the ability to laugh together enriches our connection with them.

Author Nancy Cobb's mother, an Alzheimer's patient, told her daughter of a friendship she'd formed with another Alzheimer's patient. With her trademark sense of humor, Cobb's mother described a conversation between the two new friends in which they shared *"the stories of our lives, and then, fifteen minutes later, forgot everything we said."* In that moment, "the two of us doubled up in laughter," writes Cobb.[20]

Those who care for Alzheimer's and dementia patients know the frustrations and heartache as the essence of the person they love seems to slip away. At times, thankfully, the patient's unexpected remark or gesture may help alleviate the sadness. In my hospice work, trying to become acquainted with Alzheimer's patients is like attempting to pinpoint a spirit. Who were they once? Who are they now? Is it possible to get to know someone at this stage of life?

On one visit, a patient and I perused the pages of a book of drawings by a high-fashion-shoe designer, Manolo Blahník. It was my daughter's book, and I'd brought it to the nursing home with me, hoping M. might respond; she'd mentioned once that she used to work in a nearby clothing store. I didn't know if this was true, or even if I'd heard correctly; it was difficult for her to fetch words bumping into one another in her brain. When sentences finally reached her lips, they tumbled out backward or inside out, as though her thoughts couldn't muster the strength to make the journey, so they arrived unrecognizable, in a shape that would just have to do.

Now I flipped the page to a lime green boot with a dagger of a heel.

"What do you think of this one?" I asked. The boot was lavished with a spray of peacock feathers. "Pretty wild, huh?"

"I was going to say." M.'s voice was affirming. She used the phrase repeatedly—*I was going to say*—as if my every comment were the very thought trying to navigate the pathway of her mind.

The book's oversized pages displayed shoes in styles from leopard-print to jewel-bedecked. I know nothing about high fashion, as witnessed by the fading black capris and unimaginative pink polo I was wearing. M. sported a long-sleeve-flannel dress on this sweltering July afternoon. Still, we were like two fashion critics raising an eyebrow as I offered commentary—bizarre, exotic, outrageous— and read quotes such as one by Alexandra Shulman, "If God had wanted us to wear flat shoes, he wouldn't have invented Manolo Blahník."[21]

"I was going to say," repeated M.

Finally, as I always did when it was time to leave, I

took M.'s hand.

"Is it okay if I come back to see you next week?"

"Okay," she said, smiling. Then she wagged a slender finger. "But I don't want to buy anything."

As my heart warmed with a smile, it occurred to me how little we need to know someone to receive the gift of their spirit.

"No matter what kind of life-challenging adversity people are facing, humor, like prayer, provides hope," writes Allen Klein. "In both laughter and prayer, we go beyond the world as we know it, transcending our predicament. We may not like the situation we are in, but whereas anger may draw us into our dilemma, a chuckle, like a prayer, can help us rise above it."[22]

> In both laughter and prayer, we go beyond the world as we know it, transcending our predicament.
>
> —Allen Klein

Such was the exchange — humor and prayer and hope— between a forty-seven-year old single mother who was dying of cancer and the group of women who came to pray for her. Nancy was a marketing executive who had developed a keen sense of mistrust through a series of life's betrayals. In spite of a brash approach and tough-guy exterior, her friends cherished her quick wit and sense of humor. Every week, a group of them from church would visit her home and gather around her to pray.

One member of the prayer group describes how, as death approached, Nancy's countenance appeared to soften. Each week when they returned to pray for her, she looked more radiant. Finally one of them decided to share this discovery with their friend.

"You look radiant," the woman offered one day. "Why do you think you are looking so radiant?"

"I'm looking radiant," Nancy quipped, "because I am receiving radiation."

And so Nancy's quick wittedness comforted her friends; it made them laugh. It got their attention, too, so that the words that followed, perhaps revealing the genuine source of her luminance, inspired her friends.

"You know all this business about God loving me?" she offered. "I never really believed it until now."

Ironically, the richness of feeling God's love—even in her dying—brought their friend more alive to them than they had ever known her. As if that weren't treasure enough, they went away pondering how they might live their own lives differently if they genuinely accepted God's love for them. It was a story that would later be shared at Nancy's funeral service, as friend after friend paid homage to her.

Perhaps you've experienced it yourself among a church or funeral home full of people gathered to pay last respects. During a eulogy, a memory is shared and suddenly there are smiles. Pew after pew, God's massive love radiates across the mourners. It might cause laughter or a chorus of chuckles, but either way it is cleansing; the sanctuary lights up with hope.

At the funeral of a nun, Sister Peggy, her nephew recalled the long-ago night of his grandfather's death. He had driven with two other cousins to his grandparents' house to stay with his grandmother and his aunt, Sister Peggy, as his ninety-eight-and-a-half-year-old grandfather approached death at a nearby health center. Everyone was asleep when the telephone rang at 2:00 a.m. Sister Peggy awakened and answered it, then knocked on each of the bedroom doors to deliver the sad news.

As the cousins and grandmother gathered, the telephone rang yet another time and again, Sister Peggy answered it. Again, it was the health center, this time explaining their procedure to ask the family for organ donation. Without hesitation, Sister Peggy replied, "Well, if you are able to find anything on a ninety-nine-year-old man that works better than what someone else has, you are welcome to it."

"Oh, did we laugh!" writes my nephew's wife, Linda, who attended the wake where her cousin shared this memory of their aunt. Linda's email to me includes the words *celebration* and *incredible* and *honored* and *affection* and *wonderful*, all indicative of the embrace she felt, even amidst her loss.

When God sends humor during times of grief, it seems to come with a sacred quality, as though it senses where it will be welcomed. It is often so personal to our circumstances—so uncanny in its familiarity—that we are reminded of God's role as Creator.

In my extended family, including cousins, aunts and uncles by the dozens, laughter and joking and kidding have always been as customary within our Italian heritage as were the heaping servings of homemade pasta at Sunday dinner.

It has long been a family tradition to provide three days of viewing prior to burial of the dead. I'm not sure where this ritual originated—whether its roots are ethnic or geographical—but it can be draining. Endless streams of relatives and friends show up at either of two viewings held on each of the three days, one in the afternoon, the other in the evening. Some even return again and again to pay their respects.

A pair of twins, cousins of my father, predictably showed up no matter how distant their relation to or how unacquainted they were with the deceased. *The professional mourners*, my sisters jokingly dubbed them. The two of them looked like gray-haired Italian versions of Dear Abby and Ann Landers, petite but powerful, making their entrance from the back of the funeral home, wailing and waving their white crocheted hankies, their flags of death.

"Now whose brother is he?" one would invariably ask near the casket.

When my sister Lena died, the professional mourners had long since passed away, but on the second day of viewing, two women whom none of us recognized entered the funeral home. Dressed in bulky eggplant-colored coats and toting shopping bags from Hornes, they walked side by side toward my sister's casket.

"Oh, she's beautiful!" one of them wailed.

The other tilted her head to the side. "And so young."

"What did she die of?"

One of my aunts stepped forward from a group clustered at the side of the room. "Cancer," she said sadly.

The two women shook their heads, made the sign of the cross, and on their way out the door, grabbed a handful of holy cards and threw them into their bags. We never knew who they were. But the familiarity of their unfamiliarity with the deceased resonated with us. It was a light-hearted moment in the midst of our sorrow, a bit of comic relief. God offering an insider's joke, a hug for our hearts.

Typically humor doesn't arrive the moment that grief sets in. As Klein points out, it "has to wait until after the shock has begun to subside. It has to be put on hold until after we experience, at least in some small way… that eventually everything will be all right."[23]

Solomon affirms in Ecclesiastes, "There is a time to weep and a time to laugh."[24] The beauty is that we can trust God to orchestrate the timing. There is no pressure—not even an iota— for us to determine the schedule for humor's arrival. But when humor does make an entrance, the sense of balance that accompanies it enhances well-being. Like tears, laughter is a gift from God. It is ours to accept as freely as God offers it.

"Denying grief is not healthy," adds Klein, "but neither is getting stuck in it…. Discovering a few funny moments in the midst of loss is not mocking the dead. It is honoring their memory."[25]

For Writing & Reflection

If you can think of one, write about a light-hearted moment that occurred during caregiving or after the death of
someone you loved. Recall dialogue spoken, the laughter
shared and how it made you feel.

"In the midst of winter

I found at last there was within

myself an invincible summer."

Albert Camus

five
embraced by
strength

a more
geniune self

There are times in life when we find ourselves at the stern of a situation for which we've had no prior experience. Perhaps we are taken off guard by a crisis, an emergency or a loved one's life-threatening illness. Suddenly we realize that the extent of our training included nothing more than the dispensing of aspirin or temperature-taking with a thermometer. We may have experience with another's routine hospitalization or broken limb, but what do we know about plummeting blood cell counts, oxygen concentrators or hospice services? How will we fill the potential emptiness that threatens the future?

The Bible story of David and Goliath offers an encouraging message for those of us faced with the loss of someone we love. The challenges—and they can be many—are our Goliath. The burdens of caregiving may represent an overwhelming endeavor. Or, the heartbreak and sadness may be so intense that we question our ability to survive them.

From all appearances, David didn't stand a chance against the imposing stature of the warrior Goliath. The youngest of Jesse's eight sons, David was an unassuming shepherd boy. His opponent, according to Samuel's Old Testament story, stood over nine feet tall. He wore a bronze helmet and a coat of bronze armor weighing one-hundred-twenty-six pounds. His legs were protected by bronze greaves, and a bronze javelin was slung on his back. The iron point alone of his spear shaft weighed fifteen pounds. His shield bearer accompanied him.

When David offered to represent the Israelites in an effort to single-handedly conquer Goliath, King Saul had serious doubts.

"You are not able to go out against this Philistine and fight him," Saul warned. "You are only a boy, and he has been fighting man from his youth."[26]

But David had something more powerful than Goliath's bronze armor and javelin. He knew that Goliath was not a giant from God's perspective; he understood that nothing was too big for God, and when he put his own challenge in God's hands, faithful that He would see him through, that is exactly what happened.

The God who empowered the young shepherd David

to conquer the most vicious of opponents is the same God who will get us through. The more we look to Him, the more we will see ourselves as He sees us, uncovering a truth that we are more than we ever knew.

This discovery of a deeper self may manifest itself in a quality of care that we had no idea we were capable of providing. On the surface, we worry about our technical skills, our ability to decipher medical jargon or to juggle the necessities of our own lives amidst the needs of the person dying. The list is extensive and we can choose to focus on the list (just as David might have chosen to focus on Goliath's size and armor and shield bearer) or we can turn our eyes toward God. If we choose the latter, we are sure to discover that giving care is not so much a function of what we do as much as a manifestation of who we are.

Samuel Oliver writes, "When [the] quality of care comes from the essence of who we are, a sacred union develops. Both the one being cared for and the

> **When the quality of care comes from the essence of who we are, a sacred union develops.**
> —Samuel Oliver

caregiver are transcended into a holy moment guided by the force of love."[27]

For the six months that my friend Zenta's father was in home hospice care, her mother was the primary caregiver. The bone cancer was brutal, and because Zenta's father had been intensely active in strength training, his body was able to fight the disease and live far beyond the prognosis.

"His extreme fitness was not his friend," Zenta asserts. "It was agonizing for him." Except for the twice-weekly nurse's visits, Zenta's mother fared alone.

"I had no idea how she had the strength to carry on for so long," Zenta says of her seventy-four-year-old mother. "She never had an overnight nurse. At the end, he slept on a recliner and she slept nearby on the floor tethered to him so she could feel him move, because he kept trying to get up, and he might fall and get hurt, and she was too tired to wake up without this innovation."

Zenta's mother "is amazing," according to her daughter. A World War II orphan refugee, she came to America, became a nurse, then got a bachelor's and master's degree in Russian. As caregiver, she responded in a way that drew from the essence of who she is.

Deep in our essence, a capacity to love reflects God's heart toward us. Its magnitude defies imagination. After his six-year-old son died of leukemia, author Gordon Livingston explained it this way: "Lucas evoked in me a capacity for love that I did not know I had."

Could this awareness help us grasp, in some small way, the intensity of love that God feels for us? Imagine the effect on our relationship with God if we freely accepted a love so pure and so true.

The same is true of compassion. As God is present for us, so can we show compassion for another.

"People often confuse compassion with pity," writes Dr. Sameet Kumar. "However, compassion is much more than feeling sorry for someone, or commiserating with them…it is the active alleviation of suffering by sharing your presence with someone."[28]

> " "
> At the end, he slept on a recliner and she slept nearby on the floor tethered to him so she could feel him move…
> —Zenta
> " "

As I finished typing Kumar's words, my telephone rang and I answered it. A hospice volunteer coordinator was calling to advise me that a patient I'd visited over the past few months just passed away. When I think of D., I remember her welcoming smile, the stories of missionary work that she and her late husband, a pastor, had done. As D.'s health declined, her words grew garbled and it became increasingly difficult to understand her.

On a recent visit, she lay in bed sporadically attempting to talk. As hard as I tried to listen, I had no clue what she was trying to tell me. I felt useless. In such cases, if we listen for the nudging of the Holy Spirit—call it intuition or the small voice inside, if you will—we will be guided. Finally, I took D.'s hand in mine and held it. She closed her eyes.

> ❝
> **Lucas evoked in me a capacity for love that I did not know I had.**
> —**Gordon Livingston**
> ❞

For twenty minutes, I sat at the side of her bed in silence holding her hand. Then her relatives arrived for a visit, and I prepared to leave. She opened her eyes and when I leaned over to tell her good-bye, a warm smile lit her face.

"Thank you," she whispered. In spite of my helpless feeling, my presence had been enough.

We underestimate the value of our presence. Our world is so full of doing that often we forget the treasure provided to others by just being. We do not have to fill every minute with chatting or feeding or propping the pillow; sometimes it is enough just to *be*. I encountered this insight at the bedside of another dying patient a few years ago; the patient was my mother.

At age ninety-two, Mother spent her final days in a bed at a hospice center. With her hearing aids removed, it was nearly impossible to communicate with her. Frequently she slept, peacefully for the most part. Throughout the day, my sisters and I and our husbands kept her company. When Mother did awaken, we tried to guess what might comfort her. Marge offered a sip of water. Pat brushed her hair. I decorated her shelves with flowers and family photos. One time I crawled over the bed rails to sit closer. Shuffling through her holy cards, over which she had always prayed twice daily, I read them aloud to her one at a time.

Not wanting Mother to die alone, I stayed through the night. In her room, the sofa's leather cushions were comfortable, and the staff provided me with sheets and a warm blanket. But sleep eluded me. Mother's breathing was shallow and labored. Nearby I lay motionless listening for it. Occasionally, I would rise from the sofa to replace covers Mother had kicked off or to soothe her when she seemed agitated.

It wasn't until the following night, when my thirteen-year-old joined us, that it occurred to me that my simple gesture of being there for Mother may have meant more than the holy cards, the flowers, the framed family photos. Katherine brought her sleeping bag, her laptop and a change of clothes.

"It's like a sleepover!" she offered. Now that my daughter was there, it felt like home to me. It wasn't from anything specific that Katherine said or did; it was just her presence that warmed the room. Finally it dawned on me that the same might be true for my own mother. Perhaps the familiarity of who I was—her daughter—was the best brand of comfort I could offer.

It is physically or logistically impossible, I know, for everyone to be present as a loved one dies. Yet there are so many ways we can offer the essence of who we are. Whether through prayer or meditation, by telephone or written word, if we ask, God will lead us to the way most appropriate.

One woman, who attended a reading of my first book about the loss of my father, afterwards lamented that she hadn't expressed the depth of her love for her own father before he had died. As we discussed her situation, it became apparent that it is never too late to offer words of love. In the end, she decided to express her sentiments by writing a letter to her late father, knowing that God would assure its delivery.

As we experience loss, our feelings can get so jumbled that we may be inclined to treat them like unruly children in church, shushing them or attempting to divert them. Or, as caregivers, we may let fear undermine the possibility of sharing true feelings. *Will he think I am giving up if I acknowledge that he is dying?* we wonder. *Will it make her feel worse if she sees how sad I am to lose her?*

Our charades are cloaked in good intentions, of course. We don't want to rob him of hope. Or, we don't want to scare her. On this subject, I am an expert. I come from a family of protectors, well-meaning people who suppress feelings and concoct stories, all in the name of protecting one another, as though avoiding the darkness will bring about light. And so we withhold. We downplay a dire prognosis, or hide it from those we perceive unable to handle it.

My family is resplendent with examples: the shielding of our aging mother from Dad's leukemia prognosis; the attempt to spare me, at eight months pregnant, from the news of the malignant mass on my sister's lung; my hesitation to tell my dying friend how much I would miss her for fear that she'd think I was giving up hope, and on and on and on.

"Burying our thoughts and feelings can seem like protection, but it actually leads to isolation, for both caregivers and patients," writes hospice nurse Maggie Callanan. "When families avoid being honest about what is happening, they inadvertently distance themselves emotionally from each other, which adds to their pain. Silence severs the possibility for human connection, the essential support we all need during this difficult time."[29]

The point is that speaking from the heart is one of the most comforting gifts God offers. There is no other way, I have learned, to travel through the darkness. This willingness to be transparent was one of many qualities modeled by the hospice staff involved at the end of my father's, then my mother's lives. Hospice guided us with truth, establishing an environment in which it was safe to talk about fears and ask questions that weighed on our hearts. What a shame, I mused, to save hospice solely for life's end, when the authenticity they inspired would have enhanced every stage of life.

"Dying people teach us that all any of us have is the present," writes author Sam Oliver. "People who are dying don't have time to play games, and they know when we are not being straightforward with them."[30]

When I embrace openness and become part of it, it is like slinging open a window and giving my spirit wings. It is freeing, just as it is to listen and acknowledge and forgive. At the end of my father's life, I worried and hesitated over what to say before finally discarding my fears to express the depth of my love for him and the fact that I would miss him. In doing so, I came to a new understanding of God's promise that *the truth shall set you free.*

When I think of transparency I think of my friend Mildred, an eighty-year-old with one of the most youthful and vital spirits I have ever known. Occasionally, because of her chronological age and various health issues, Mildred shares her feeling that death may not be far in the future for her.

One evening, she told the five of us who comprise a prayer group with her that her son Paul had already written her eulogy, and he gave it to her to read. The first time she read it, she said, she cried. The second time she laughed, as she relished her son's description of the many various recipes with which she'd experimented in her attempts at making meatloaf. Now as we sat in her living room with our cups of tea, Mildred motioned toward a small wooden box crafted by another of her four sons and displayed near the fireplace.

"They can't use the box Craig made to bury me in the church garden," Mildred lamented.

"Why?" we asked.

"Because it must be biodegradable."

"Hey, can we split you up?" our friend Kim offered,

her unique perspective always lighting the room. "Must all your remains remain together?"

It struck me how fluidly the discussion flowed between Mildred and her sons and, later, among the women of our prayer group, about a subject that many people attempt to avoid. Her sons adore Mildred, as do those of us privileged to call her our friend, and the idea of losing her is devastating. But her openness inspires the same in us. Because of it, we are able to share heartfelt conversation, light heartedness and love.

Surviving loss means facing the profound absence of a loved one. At times the heartache seems unbearable. God uses our strengths—whatever they may be—to get us through. We are guided to the right path by the God who knows us, the God who created us. We can be comforted by the Old Testament's suggestion to "Trust in the Lord with all your heart and lean not on your own understanding; in all your ways acknowledge Him, and He will make your paths straight."[31] The self we encounter along the way is genuine, a self we can recognize as a manifestation of His perfect love.

For Writing & Reflection

Make a list of gifts that make you who you are. How can you draw upon those gifts to navigate the pathways of loss?

"The community needs the dying

to make it think of the eternal and

to make it listen."

Dr. Cicely Saunders, Founder
St. Christopher Hospice, London

six
embraced by
faith

a bridge
to God

When someone close to us is dying, we start thinking more earnestly about what happens next. Where are we headed after life here on earth? Whom will we meet there? In this way, people who are dying connect us to the spiritual realm. It is as if a door has opened that we barely dared peek through before. The "peace that passes all understanding" results from the realization that the God we had hoped to find is there for us, arms opened wide, generous with compassion. My friends Mike and Brie encountered this very embrace even as they suffered the heartbreaking loss of their newborn son.

"Mike, it doesn't look good," Brie said. Propped against pillows in the hospital bed, she was holding Luke, their baby boy born four short hours earlier. "He's slipping away."

From the day Brie had had the second of two devastating ultrasounds, twenty weeks into her pregnancy, she and Mike had feared the worst.

"I'm sorry to tell you that your child has a lethal condition," the doctor had said. "The child may survive the pregnancy in the womb, but at birth ..."

"It's 100% certain your child will not survive," another doctor affirmed.

Still, wanting to give their unborn son every possible chance, they opted to continue the pregnancy, praying for a miracle. Well-intended strangers, unaware that the couple was grieving an impending loss, would congratulate them or ask about the due date or the baby's gender. Finally, Brie stopped having ultrasounds; the diagnosis was clear, and, with each additional test, the results were "like a slap in the face," she remembers. "The same bad news."

Now after months of hoping and praying and grieving, Luke lay dying in his mother's arms.

"It was one of the saddest moments of our lives," Mike remembers, fighting back tears. "But it was also a beautiful time. There was an amazing sense of peace. He was passing to eternity and it's almost like his life was a bridge to God."

"I think because he was our son, and we were holding him as he was going from this world to heaven," explains Brie, "we felt like heaven was so close. Like God was right there underneath all of us, holding all of us."

In the Old Testament, Isaiah writes that "on those living in the land of the shadow of death a light has dawned."[32] Of course, we are all "living in the land of the shadow of death," but I wonder this: do those who are closer to death see the light more brightly? Have they been chosen to deliver a message of hope to the rest of us?

> **❝**
> **There was an amazing sense of peace. He was passing to eternity and it's almost like his life was a bridge to God.**
> **—Mike**
> **❞**

When it was decided that her leukemia stricken father would be removed from life support, a woman named Meagan flew from Philadelphia to Seattle to be with him. Her sister flew from California.

That evening a Nor'easter struck, and Meagan's flight was the only one out of Philadelphia that was not cancelled. The ticket she had secured, in fact, was for the last available seat and she was grateful to have it, as many were stranded on the East coast looking for any way out.

The next morning in their father's hospital room,

Meagan recalls a persistent "feeling that there was a 'presence' in the room with us, specifically in the upper left corner, from my dad's perspective; it was over my back right shoulder."

Meagan and her sister visited with their father, said their good-byes, and with great sadness, returned to his room after the life support systems had been removed.

"My sister and I both took one of his hands in ours and held them as he took his last breaths," Meagan recalls.

> **I have no doubt that God's angels were waiting to escort him to Heaven ...**
>
> —Meagan

"He opened his eyes and looked directly up to the left corner of the room, and was gone from earth. I have no doubt in my mind that God's angels were waiting to escort him to Heaven; I could feel it and he could see it."

Many people, with varying degrees of faith, describe an affirmation of faith unexpectedly arising above sorrow. The sense of God's presence can be so palpable that the message is unmistakable: *I will never let you face this enormous loss alone.* For Meagan, watching her father pass so peacefully and experiencing God's presence helped allay her own fears about dying and strengthened her belief that, no matter what the situation, God would see her through.

Some survivors recall an occurrence surrounding the moment of death whose unique nature is so appropriate to the person dying that the relevance seems like a whisper of reassurance, instilling a sense of peace.

Until my friend Zenta's father died of bone cancer, he was a vital seventy-seven-year-old whose adamant devotion to strength training kept him as physically fit as men half his age. At the end, Zenta and her mother were at his side.

"Just as he passed, a fiery sun set over the wetlands which his home overlooks," recalls Zenta. "A short while later, a full moon rose over the ocean. Perfect symbolism and perfect symmetry. As an English professor, he would have appreciated that."

Some occurrences surrounding the approaching death seem to have a supernatural essence, similar to the presence Meagan sensed in her dying father's hospital room. Many recall their loved one reaching out from the hospital bed, as though responding to a spirit in another world. It is not unusual for the dying to utter names of those gone before, as though approaching the receiving line of a heavenly welcoming committee. Others have described a breeze ushering through the room or a flicker of light suddenly emanating from the ceiling. We may never know the physical explanation of these mysterious occurrences, if there is one, but for those of faith, they offer a sense of peace.

"Simply pondering our life's questions leads us into a dimension of ourselves where only our spirit can travel," observes author and pastor Sam Oliver. "Here, we experience freedom to incarnate into our daily lives an infinite array of choices."[33]

A nurse named Victoria recalls the chemistry she felt, as a graduate nurse, with a middle-aged Jewish patient who was dying of ovarian cancer in a Philadelphia hospital. Although the two women came from different faith backgrounds, they both related to God, Victoria explains, and shared deep and meaningful conversations about their faith.

"Prior to her death, we talked about how she wanted me to say a prayer upon her death," Victoria remembers. "I did say this prayer, a Jewish prayer, blessing her life here on earth and hoping that she'd be in God's hands upon her death. It was some type of ritual she'd had within her family. I was alone with her and held her hand when I said it."

As Victoria describes what happened next, her voice grows intense; the experience still, after nearly three decades, fills her with emotion. She explains that the patient's room, in an older part of the hospital, had windows that were basically nailed shut; they had some type of screening on them, she remembers.

"Upon her death," Victoria says, "the windows opened up and there was a brisk air flow through that entire room and it was the most peaceful feeling...They flung open, and they shut. I stood there in amazement. I still get chills— in a good way— thinking about it.

"There was no explanation except God. Would anybody believe me?" she asks in a way that indicates the answer doesn't matter. "There was that fresh breeze, with the windows open, as though God swirled into the room and left. It was so peaceful. I knew it was of God, nothing evil or scary. I never pursued what caused it; I just knew it was God and that was it. I didn't need any explanation. It was definitely strengthening."

We may all have different ideas of what happened that day in the hospital room, as Victoria bade good-bye to her patient. As Oliver states, "In the conceptual world, we can find explanations for what happened. In the eyes of faith, the possibilities go beyond our perceptions. Through the eyes of faith, incredible grace becomes possible."[34]

Some survivors experience grace upon looking back at a comment or gesture their loved one made during his or her final hours and discovering in it a clue of the impending departure. It is as if the bridge to God stands firm and, in recognizing this, the dying person felt safe enough to cross it.

> **It was definitely strengthening.**
> —Victoria

My friend Jim recalls the bittersweet memory of his cherished ninety-four-year-old mother displaying her readiness for the journey.

Jim's parents, Adeline and Charlie, "had been very social people who loved going to parties with their many friends," according to their only son. After his father's death, Jim, his wife and two children included Adeline in their trips to Disney World, shared holidays with her and kept her involved in their daily lives, not out of a sense of obligation, but because "she was fun to be around and made everything more enjoyable."

Eventually, Adeline suffered a fall that resulted in a broken hip, surgery and a move to her retirement community's nursing home where she began experiencing swallowing difficulties. Her family was faced with the gut-wrenching decision of whether or not to authorize a feeding tube. With it, she would live bedridden or wheelchair-bound in a nursing home, fighting periodic infections, and the fact was that her living will had requested no extraordinary efforts to keep her alive. Without it, she would starve to death. After a visit one night they left tearful, knowing that by the next morning, a decision was needed.

Earlier that day, Adeline had asked her caregiver to take her in the wheelchair to the nursing home beauty parlor to get her hair done. "On the way," Jim remembers, "the nurses kidded her, asking why she needed to get her hair done. She replied with a big smile, 'I'm going to a party with Charlie.' That night she died. The official cause was aspirational pneumonia; we feel certain she willed it. She was ready and had no fear."

> **She was ready and had no fear.**
>
> —Jim

What a gift Adeline left behind for Jim and his family!

"It was as though my mother had taken control and spared us from the trauma of having to make such an unfair decision," Jim says. And even more, Adeline's words, "I'm going to a party with Charlie," gave her family the peace of mind of knowing that she was looking forward to a reunion with her beloved husband, headed for a place at which she looked forward to arriving.

Because the grief journey is complex, the idea of finding peace may, at first, not seem plausible. Not only is there heartache to face, there can also be healthcare to orchestrate, funerals to arrange, bills to pay, estates to settle. On top of it all, things will go wrong—the obstacles of everyday life—and push one to the limits.

Recently my family's eight-year-old golden retriever had surgery for the removal of a bad oral tumor. Unable to remove the entire growth, which was too invasive, the veterinarian was not optimistic. We waited anxiously for the biopsy results, and finally we received them. It turned out that Sammi had fibersarcoma, an aggressive form of cancer. Anyone who views a pet as a family member can imagine the shock of learning that the dog they perceived to be perfectly healthy has somewhere between a week and a month to live. We were devastated.

On the day that we received the biopsy report, my computer printer jammed. I tried in my inept way to fix it, but nothing I did worked, so I decided to turn it off. On the screen, the words "shutting down" froze. No matter how many times I poked the "off" button, those words stayed frozen there—*shutting down*—as if I needed a re-minder of our impending loss! If I were the violent type, I would have thrown a lamp at it.

That same night my husband tried to set his digital alarm clock for an early morning men's meeting he attends weekly. But the alarm refused to be set. Each time Randy entered the wake-up time, the numbers on the screen reverted to the current time. And each time they did, he grew angrier. He fidgeted and fiddled until he took the clock into the bathroom and spoke ugly words to it.

During that same time, in the spirit of making the most of Sammi's last days, Katherine took her outside to play in twelve inches of newly fallen snow. Like many teenagers clinging to cell phones, she tucked hers into her coat pocket, setting it on "vibrate." When she came inside, she noticed her lifeline to her social world missing. We spent hours raking through snow in search of it, even with flashlights in the darkness of night. It was nowhere to be found.

It is hard to deal with the notion of loss, in whatever way we choose to deal with it, and simultaneously feel badgered by an onslaught of injustices. A plethora of clichés comes to mind: the last straw, insult added to injury. They are enough to provoke a shaking fist at God, a cry of unfairness.

At first glance, we may view these occurrences as the *opposite* of grace. Torture to hearts already riddled with grief. But as time goes by, we may gain a new perspective on the glitches that taunt us. Might a non-functioning computer printer, for example, be an invitation to an afternoon away from the desk, a few relaxed hours simply savoring the short time remaining with a beloved pet?

Could the refusal of an alarm clock to be set for an early wake-up offer a chance to gain rest in a stressful time of sadness?

Might the absence of disruptive phone calls and text messages enhance the quality of time left for a teenager and her dying dog?

Is it possible that these annoyances were grace showing up in disguise?

We may not recognize minor setbacks as gifts at the moment they occur, and perhaps they will never be more than the aggravation they provoke. But by making an effort to open our hearts to possibilities, we may find compassion waiting to embrace us.

So how do we make this connection with God, the ultimate source of peace? What can we do to experience a sense of calm amidst the turmoil? Is not this the very possibility at the heart of the Psalmist's words, "Be still and know that I am God?"

"We are not forced to take wings to find Him," affirmed Teresa of Avila, "but have only to seek solitude and to look within ourselves."

After my mother's death, I sat in a chair doing nothing, the way Mother used to sit in our gray living room chair, her feet propped on the matching ottoman, staring out the window beyond the breezeway's terra cotta tile floor. It bothered me, as a child, to see her sitting there as though her life had no purpose.

"I will never sit in a chair and do nothing," I promised myself.

Twelve days after Mother's death, I was still sitting there. Alone. Dangling. Briefly I turned on the television. At 8:46 a.m., the minute the first plane had crashed into the World Trade Center five years before, a bell rang in commemoration. Family members read the victims' names. Grief upon grief, layers of sorrow. The enormity of loss was suffocating, conjuring up the billows of smoke that had risen from Ground Zero. I flicked off the power.

After six years of tending to Mother's needs, as many caregivers discover, it was as if a volcano had erupted from the confusion that was my world, and I was too weary to crawl out of the crater. The debris from dealing with Mother's dementia and other complications, her numerous moves through continuing care, and a whole plethora of medical, logistical and relational issues, lay in heaps around me.

Yet in this same solitude, I have discovered the sacred space where I can go to meet my God. For me, the connection is pronounced when I gaze upon the mountains and sense the enormity of God's love. Here, a cluster of leaves outside the window is tinged maroon, hinting of autumn's return. The chair in which I sit offers comfort; my feet are propped on the ottoman. The room holds memories of Mother: a pair of botanical prints that once decorated her apartment, another piece depicting roses cascading from an awning-covered window box, a lamp from her nightstand. Gifts, of course, as is this place, but nothing like the one she did not know she left.

I have come to love the stillness. The calm of sitting in the quiet of God's revelation, a God who each day, it seems, I am beginning anew to know.

Your space may be at a lake or near the ocean or looking out the living room window. The gift of grace is there.

"If we are children of God," writes Oswald Chambers, "we have tremendous treasure in nature and will realize that it is holy and sacred. We will see God reaching out to us in every wind that blows, every sunrise and sunset, every cloud in the sky, every flower that blooms, and every leaf that fades..."[35]

In the throes of grief, it may seem that we will never find peace again. The truth is, if we depend entirely on ourselves, we may not. The dying forge a bridge to the ultimate source of peace. God waits with open arms to share a sense of calm. Find a chair. Relax. Close your eyes, or look out on God's natural world. Take a deep breath. And allow yourself to be embraced by grace.

For Reflection & Writing

Think about Psalm 46:10, "Be still, and know that I am God." What does this mean to you and how might it apply to your life?

"Night is more alive and

richly colored than day."

Vincent vanGogh

seven
embraced by
art

the angel
in the marble

Sometimes I wonder if God created art for the purpose of soothing our souls. Indeed, from ancient dances and sacred diagrams to modern-day psychotherapeutic applications, creative expression and enjoyment have played significant roles in healing. Research indicates that the arts go so far as to stimulate improvements of immune functioning and decreased blood pressure.

The key, writes Sandra Bertman, a pioneer in the use of arts in grief counseling, is that art helps us to "relieve, to re-live, to relevé (from the French, in ballet, to rise above, to stand on one's toes)...to transcend."[36]

What is it about art that helps us transcend our sorrows?

One of its mysteries, it seems to me, lies in the fact that at the same time that we yield to it, it liberates us. A contradiction perhaps, but is not this the miracle of faith itself? Likewise, people speak of losing themselves in the music or letting the prose lead the way. Coleridge described the reader's temporary "suspension of disbelief" when immersed in fiction.

With art, we are taken to places we never knew existed. Here we can explore and find meaning. Here our hearts may wander and sense and discover. How liberating it can be to step out of the world, not to escape it, but into a deeper connection with the soul! Making this connection unleashes emotion, including sorrow. Art helps us do this with tenderness.

"I saw the angel in the marble and carved until I set him free," said 16th Century Italian artist Michelangelo. Burdened with sadness, lost in confusion, hardened by numbness, are we not ourselves the angels in the marble? Deep in our souls, we yearn to be set free. Art is a gift—whether practiced or partaken of—that touches the heart and nurtures.

My godson Peter, when he was twenty-seven-years old, had just returned home from his new job the day he learned of his beloved grandfather's death. He doesn't remember the details of the telephone call, who delivered the news or what they said, though he believes it must have been his mother. What he does remember, in detail, is what he did next.

In his apartment's front room, he picked up his guitar

and clicked the amp's power switch. Just like an old radio, Peter explains, it takes a moment for a tube amplifier to heat up. Typically, he would strum the guitar strings while the amp's power tubes prepared to drive the speaker, rendering a weak, tinny sound. Today though, he waited in forlorn silence. When the speaker came to life, he dialed up the volume. The speaker's hiss told him the music would be too loud for an apartment, but he didn't care. Let the downstairs neighbors take a broom to their ceiling.

With pick in hand, Peter ripped into the opening notes of *Hide Away*, an instrumental blues song written and originally recorded by Freddie King, though it was Eric Clapton's rendition that especially inspired him. As he began to play, "the tubes in the amp pressed into a warm overdrive and the sound reverberated around the small room," he remembers.

"I can always play the first couple of minutes of *Hide Away* like Eric, but at the point in the song where his playing becomes dense with improvisation, I just make it up on my own. Sometimes it yawns, and other times it sounds all right. But on this day, it was beautiful. A creative power took over," Peter recalls.

"As I turned the corner to head into the solo, I played notes that I could not even recognize as mine. My heart

> ## A creative power took over ... the music was a gift.
> —Peter

weighed against my chest, and my emotions were running well ahead of my thoughts. I just lost my grandpap, and I love him more than I can express with words. I wasn't even ready to cry for him. But the music was a gift.... It was a rough day after the phone call, and an even more painful night. But as I played *Hide Away*, God reminded me that He is with me, and Grandpap is with Him."

In the midst of heartache, Peter felt God's embrace. He transcended his grief to experience God's peace. *Out of darkness, God created light.* The music was a gift that helped penetrate the darkness, revealing a view of God's love and enabling the connection.

Reflecting on faith and art, author Madeleine L'Engle writes of returning to childhood with its high level of creativity expressed from a place of inner truth. This place—where we feel uninhibited and without constraint—can function as a much-needed respite for those shouldering the weight of grief.

"In art," L'Engle writes, "we are once again able to

do all the things we have forgotten; we are able to walk on water; we speak to the angels who call us; we move, unfettered, among the stars."[37]

A long sequence of circumstances, replete with God's grace, brought my dying father to a hospice bed in the sunroom of my home where he spent the last nine days of his life. Each night as I lay upstairs trying to fall asleep, I could barely entertain the gravity of the circumstances.

My father is in my sunroom dying. The thought repeatedly echoed in my mind. It was one of the saddest truths I had ever faced but strangely, it also contained an inherent richness. Something more

> "
> **In art, we are once again able to do all the things we have forgotten; we are able to walk on water; we speak to the angels who call us; we move unfettered among the stars.**
> —Madeleine L'Engle
> "

spectacular than death itself was happening here, something sprouting from my belief that the death of Jesus Christ led to a resurrection, that life is eternal. Finally one day, I picked up a tablet and pen. I was sitting on a chair in the corner of the sunroom alone with Dad who was sleeping. And I began to write.

My father is in my sunroom dying. You cannot tell me that God did not script this scene. Ceiling fan twirling in rhythm to the oxygen concentrator, chugging, spitting, chugging, spitting.

Five arched windows, each with twenty panes, frame a close-up of Armstrong pines. Hollyhocks inch toward their second bloom: blood reds, pinks, peaches. Renovations to this room, formerly my husband's graphic design studio, were completed barely three months ago. Built-in desks ripped out, computers and printers relocated, fax and photocopier removed just in time to accommodate, unbeknownst to us, a divine schedule for set design: a Turkish rug—periwinkle, salmon and tan—a striped, deep-seat sofa with floral cushions, matching ottoman, and two new chairs, one for the hospice nurse to keep watch through the night shift, the other for us to take turns sitting next to Dad and holding his hand. [38]

A couple of months after Dad was gone, I returned to those words. They did not erase my grief, but they offered me comfort. So I continued writing. The more I wrote, the more I recognized the tenderness with which God had accompanied me through my final summer with Dad. The writing became a vehicle across pathways toward deeper truths.

Writing, of course, happens to be my profession and,

in this case, it led to my first book, a memoir. God used it to help me heal from one of the deepest losses I had known. Just as music provided a way for Peter to enter grief and encounter God's embrace, writing has unveiled God's love for me.

We don't have to write books or play the guitar or paint masterpieces to discover the solace so generously imbued in the arts. We don't need to carry a tune or hold the paintbrush or perform the ballet. Though some of us may choose to engage actively in expressing ourselves, many prefer retreating into the worlds of others by visiting galleries, reading memoirs, or attending films, for example. Still others welcome the sense of community, perhaps by sharing stories and dialogue as members of a group or anonymously on the Internet. No matter how we experience it, art can reach through grief, offering the sense of a compassionate presence.

In the early September, 2005 wake of hurricane Katrina, grief-stricken crowds of New Orleans residents witnessed the greatest loss many of them had ever encountered. Author and music therapist Dr. Joy S. Berger recalls Harry Connick, Jr. singing Louis Armstrong's classic *Do You Know What It Means to Miss New Orleans*, as residents left the city on bus after bus.

He sang it, says Berger, "to the world for his hometown, his family (his father had been mayor) and his dispersed community."[39] Poignant, to be sure. And through the stir of music God whispered, *Your heartbreak is my heartbreak. I am with you.*

Author Nancy Cobb illustrates a similar embrace when her mother, stricken with Alzheimer's, was dying in a Connecticut hospice. Singer Peter Yarrow, whose mother had died in the same hospice facility, returned to serenade the patients there. Cobb was visiting her mother at the time, and later wrote this about it.

I crouch down beside her and whisper, "Mom, Peter Yarrow is going to sing. Remember, Peter, Paul, and Mary— that first album—we knew every song." My mother moves her lips as if to speak, but no sound comes out. Then Peter is singing. "Weave, weave, weave me the sunshine..." and I begin to cry and I can't stop. The tears I've held in all week spill out over my mother's bedclothes; I'm taken over by wracking, body-quaking sobs. I try to sing along to my mother, but I choke on the words. Music is always an emotional catalyst, but this music, folk music, skids right past my head and cracks open my heart. I cry through song after song, until suddenly Peter is saying, "I'm going to sing one more." Panicked, a voice   actually, a squeak   emerges. "Will you take a request?" I say through tears.

"Well … um…what is it?" he asks patiently, though I can tell he'd rather not. By this time I must look like a deranged raccoon, bleary-eyed, mascara run amok, but I don't care. Weakly, with all the hope in the world, I say, "'Blowin' in the Wind'?"

He smiles. "Just what I was going to sing," he says.

We smile at each other. Then we both nod in mutual amazement, and say, simultaneously, "Synchronicity."

Honest to God.

So he starts to sing "Blowin' in the Wind" and then he walks toward me, and my mother is moving her lips again—I've got to believe she's trying to sing—until he is beside us. I trust he knows what's going on because he's been through the same thing himself in this very same place. Then he stops playing the guitar and takes my hand and takes my mother's hand, and now he's singing to us a cappella, which really gets me, and he sings the last three verses like this, with no accompaniment except the audience singing softly in the background, and in the foreground he continues to hold our hands and sing from what seems like the center of his being, binding us together into the oddest, most perfect little trio.

In a novel this would seem contrived, but I'll tell you, being there in that room filled with sunshine, with Peter Yarrow serenading my dying mother was, considering the circumstances, about as good as it gets.[40]

These moments of compassionate connection can be experienced at such a deep level that they seem to define a type of spiritual communion. In art's welcoming embrace, we find ourselves in the company of God.

The gift of art is so generous that in practicing it ourselves, if we choose to do so, it doesn't even matter how lacking in skills we are. I think of the blankets and scarves and slippers I have knitted through the years. Without fail, my finished pieces are uneven or riddled with holes from dropped stitches, barely worthy of being worn or displayed (though my young granddaughters find creative uses for them). But it is in the doing, the rhythm of the needles clicking, the rows of increasing stitches, the quiet sitting, that I find peace.

So also it is with any art we choose. To use another as an example, expressive writing is readily available and requires no experience or special tools.

An accomplished businessman, not one to engage in emotional displays, shared the experience of losing his mother in answer to my email soliciting stories of loss. In a cover note, his words reflected those of many others who shared their stories, as well.

"Much to my surprise," he shared, "when I started writing it down, it felt good. I didn't plan to write so much, but once I got started I couldn't stop."

Author Martha Whitmore Hackman, who filled four notebooks with entries after her daughter's death, says, "The important thing for most of us is not that we have made something of artistic value, but that we have taken a grief that lies like a lump against our hearts, and moved it away from us."[41]

> 66
> **Much to my surprise ... when I started writing it down, it felt good.**
> 99

The benefits of expressive writing have been compared to those of receiving therapy, to being able to voice our "feelings and judgments to a sympathetic ear, to someone who won't turn on the ballgame or do the dishes, won't cradle the phone, multi-task, and tune you out. We usually have to pay for that kind of focused attention," asserts author Henriette Klauser. She notes that the professional counselor's job is to lead us to answers inside of ourselves, the answers we already know, but don't know that we know.[42]

Professional therapy can result in significant strides toward emotional healing, and the suggestion to engage in personal writing is not to replace or diminish that value.

But, for some, writing can fill an important role.

"The world is impatient," notes Klauser. "It tells you, *You should be over that by now.* The page does not judge how long it takes you. The page can hold your sorrow and will not rush you on."[43]

But how do we find the words? What do we write? I have found that one of writing's most treasured gifts is wrapped in the details. None of us has to be an expert to collect, make lists of or jot down details that we recall. Like knitting another stitch onto the needle, each detail contributes to the fabric of healing.

In writing workshops for the bereaved, I sometimes encourage participants to list details they recall about those whose loss they mourn. Usually I offer a passage as inspiration, such as this one that Kay Gibbons wrote about her mother.

She was a good country woman. She kept crocheted doilies pinned to the backs and arms of chairs. She could snap a live chicken's neck quick as a wink, and clean and dress the thing in time for supper. She was lighting the pilot light in the oven when they announced John F. Kennedy was dead, and she sat right down on the kitchen floor and cried. That was the first time I realized she thought of things besides hot breakfasts, sterile Mason jars, quilts, and the square of clay dirt we tried to farm.[44]

As they put their own recalled details to paper, some workshop participants shed tears or lean elbows on the table, foreheads into hands. Others smile. The emotions, I believe, are similar to those we experience when we happen upon an old snapshot. Depending on where we are on our path of grieving, we may react differently to the exact same snapshot on one day versus another. The important thing is that getting emotions out in the open can trigger healing.

Writing down details of the loss *experience* can also help in this regard. The details of first hearing the prognosis. The irritating questions posed by an in-law. Or the details surrounding the awareness of death.

For example, I will never forget returning home on a cloudy Saturday afternoon when my teenage daughter rose from the sofa, her face tear-stained, her eyes filled with compassion. Standing there clutching a John Wanamaker's bag with a new pair of blue jeans inside, I knew at once that my cancer-stricken best friend had died while I was out shopping.

Or the following year on the night before Thanksgiving. After traveling four hours to the Pittsburgh hospital where my oldest sister was a cancer patient, my husband, my daughters and I arrived simultaneous to another sister and her daughter coming from New Jersey. Together we rode the elevator to the oncology floor, anxious to see Lena; it had been almost a month since we'd last visited. But when we arrived at her door, there in my sister's room was nothing more than a bouquet of deflated balloons dangling above her empty bed.

By pushing these memories onto the page, I allow myself sadness. In doing so, a burden lifts from my heart, one of God's many strategies for offering comfort.

This is not to suggest that writing, or any other art, will eradicate our pain. That is not the role it plays. As Author William Loizeau whose daughter, Anna, died at only five-and-a-half-months old, explains, "I recall a wild need to set things down, to grasp with words what had gone from my hands, though the words seemed—they still seem—so inadequate."[45]

For many years, my friend Howard has taught writing at a university. He also facilitates writing groups for women who had cancer. He points out, "No magic bullets here. No 'Write three paragraphs and you'll feel all better in the morning.' Words are not miracle cures. But writing—not talking about something, not thinking about something—can help someone who's hurting make it through the day. And the day after that. And the day after that."

Having had more than one-hundred skin cancers re-moved, Howard has used his own writing to help deal with the pain and stress.

"Though none has been life-threatening," he writes, "each surgery has taken away both a small piece of my skin and a small part of my spirit.

"Somewhere around the fortieth surgery, I started to write about my feelings," he recalls. "I wrote a play about how unsettling it was to constantly have pieces of my body cut away and dozens of stitches put in. That helped me bring the feelings out of the shadows and into the sunlight where I could see them more clearly."

Seeing more clearly offers a sense of calm. In my own experience with grief, I have discovered that calmness is a precious commodity.

In *Riding the Dog*, I recount a chaotic trip my sister and I made to Florida in an effort to fulfill our father's final requests, to retrieve legal papers from a bank safe deposit box and to host a farewell dinner party on his behalf for his friends. After leaving the party, in a mad dash to the airport, we got lost. We were trying to catch an earlier flight home having received a frantic call from another sister who was at our father's bedside.

When we finally were aboard, I pulled out the spiral-bound tablet I had kept throughout Dad's illness. This was the tablet on which I'd jotted down instructions for operating the oxygen concentrator, the names of hospice caregivers, a to-do list for our Florida trip. And now I used it to write. The act of writing, as described in the following passage, granted me reprieve.

> *The pen in my hand fills the empty pages of my spiral-bound tablet. It takes on a life of its own, recounting my escapade at safe deposit box #447…the bittersweetness of meeting Dad's friends.*
>
> *In the spotlight of the overhead bulb, the pen takes me into uncharted waters. It writes words to speak in Dad's memory at a funeral I can hardly bear to think about. It is as if the pen takes charge so I don't have to. It writes and writes and writes….*
>
> *The tablet is almost full. The pen writes on the backs of sheets now, up the margins of the pages willy-nilly, wherever there is space. The pages are out of order, but the pen does not care. It cannot stop writing. It has to write.*
>
> *Until finally, ever so politely, the pen stops. It stops and rests on the tablet, giving me the chance just to sit. In my tiredness, it feels as if someone is cradling me. As if God is wrapping me in peace. Helping me to breathe. Breathe, breathe.* [46]

Sometimes the ability to breathe is all that our writing

will have to offer. And sometimes, the ability to breathe is exactly what we need.

Your gift might be found in sculpting or in painting or on the pages of a scrapbook or on stage at the performing arts center. Art is there for all of us to enjoy. It doesn't matter whether your hands are dancing across the piano keys or whether you are settling into a chair to adjust the headphones. Open the gift. It has been chosen for you with love.

For Writing and Reflection

Intentionally allocate time to visit your local art museum, take in a play or simply relax while listening to music. Afterwards, write down any emotions you experienced. Or, settle in with some photos of your loved one, making a list of details illustrating his or her character.

"One who has journeyed

in a strange land cannot

return unchanged."

C. S. Lewis

eight
embraced by
wisdom

the rest of
the ride

P eople often ask me how I can bear working with hospice patients, getting to know the dying in their final days only to face the inevitable loss.

"Doesn't it pull you down?" a friend recently wanted to know.

I wish there were a succinct and comprehensible answer to the question. One that doesn't sound schmaltzy or smack of cliché. For yes, the sting of heartbreak abounds, and more times than I can count, my eyes have burned with tears upon answering the telephone to discover that the sun has set on a new and cherished relationship as quietly as it had risen. Certainly the sense of loss is not as personal as that precipitated by the death of my own relatives or friends with whom I've shared more of life than solely the end of it. But sharing the end of life's journey, no matter the length of the acquaintanceship, can be life-changing. For loss gives us the chance to look at life in a way that only those who are losing it can provide. It is a perspective that can illuminate our own journey...the rest of the ride, so to speak. This kind of luminescence amid the darkness has a sacred quality to it, as though God is lighting a candle.

"The experience of loss itself does not have to be the defining moment of our lives," wrote author Gerald Sittser. "Instead, the defining moment can be *our response* to the loss. It is not what happens *to* us that matters as much as what happens *in* us."[47]

Many who travel through grief learn life-enriching lessons. The lessons may be garnered from the admirable qualities of the person we are losing or have lost: the way they model how to face adversity, for instance. Or, as we witness the brevity of their remaining days, we may become more conscious of time and more deliberate about how we choose to spend it.

> "
> It is not what happens to us that matters as much as what happens in us.
> —Gerald Sittser
> "

Having not experienced dying from the patient's point of view, I dare not pontificate about the attitude any of us might or might not project from our deathbeds. But I do know this. I have had the honor of accompanying patients who have greeted death with more grace and dignity than I have exhibited over losing my way on a road trip. Certainly there is a message in this, delivered so tenderly that surely God is the sender.

A. was an eighty-seven-year-old hospice patient, one of many who exemplified facing adversity with grace. The first time I entered her nursing home room, I stood at the side of her bed where she lay sleeping. Even with her eyes closed, A.'s face was gentle, yet self-assured. She must have sensed my presence, because she awoke, revealing crystal blue eyes filled with vigor, and before I could introduce myself as her hospice visitor, this is what she said: "I had the most wonderful day yesterday!"

"Really?" I asked.

"Yes," she said. "I was sleeping, and when I woke up, there was my old college roommate sitting at my bedside! I thought it was a mirage, but it wasn't. We had such a lovely visit."

"What did you talk about?" I asked.

"Oh, everything. Music, books. She is a wonderful musician, a pianist. She inspired a love of music in me."

And so this woman who was dying of heart failure "had the most wonderful day yesterday." I loved her immediately. Often, at the end of our visits, A. would put her arms around me. She would sing "I love you a bushel and a peck," engaging me in a sway as she recalled every verse to the song.

The last words I heard A. speak were in prayer one overcast afternoon as she and I held hands. She thanked God for giving her a life filled with joy and said she couldn't imagine living without it. She prayed on and on, as though the brief moments left in her life could barely hold her gratitude.

Later, when her daughter told me A.'s childhood story, the lesson of her God-focused attitude grew even more poignant. A. had been one of eleven siblings, the third to the youngest. At age thirteen, she and some of her sisters and brothers arrived home from school one day to find their house burned to the ground. They didn't know where their parents were. Though her parents had survived the fire, A. was sent to live with an older brother, never to return to her mother's arms. Her mother died before A. was married. Throughout her life, her daughter told me, A. carried a longing for her mother.

A.'s is the story I recall when people ask if working with the dying pulls me down. In spite of her own life difficulties, even in the face of death, she shared joy with others as though she had plenty to spare. Hers is a life lesson that enriches me. It lifts me up. It has been an honor—

there is no other way to describe it—to walk alongside A. and so many other patients, even for brief stints, on their journeys.

The wisdom to be garnered from the dying can emanate from their very spirit, as was the case for me with A. At other times, their messages are pointed and delivered with a sense of urgency. At this crucial time in life's journey, the dying often gain a new or sharper perspective, and they may feel compelled to share their insights. Perhaps it is their proximity to the Creator that persuades us to listen.

My friend Noah recalls a time when he was a young pastor visiting a hospitalized man, a well-known poet in the community, who was seriously ill.

"In our conversation," Noah remembers, "he asked me how things were going for me. Since we were having an honest conversation and sharing freely, I shared with him that I was going through a rough time. I was tired and weary of my responsibilities and the expectations people had of me as a pastor. Sometimes I felt like walking away.

"He looked intently at me, pushed himself up from his hospital bed with his elbows and said, 'Young man, preach hope to your people. It's the only thing you have left when everything else is gone.'

> ❝
>
> I often draw
> from that well
> of wisdom ...
> I can always
> speak of and pray
> for hope.
>
> —Noah
>
> ❞

"I often draw from that well of wisdom," writes Noah, "especially in difficult times or for others to whom I minister. If I have done all that I can do, and said all that I know to say, and feel that I have come to an empty place, I can always speak of and pray for hope."

In this way, the dying introduce us to new realizations about what is important in life. Suddenly time seems precious, a perspective we gain from those who have little of it left.

Author Anne Lamott, in an *O Magazine* article, writes of becoming more aware of the fact that she is not going to live forever. This truth, she says, has actually set her free. She tells this story.

"Eleven years ago, when my friend Pammy was dying at the age of thirty-seven, we went shopping at Macy's. She was in a wheelchair, with a wig and three weeks to live. I tried on a short dress and came out to model it for Pammy. I asked if she thought it made me look big in the thighs, and she said, so kindly, 'Annie? You just don't have that kind of time.' I live by this story."[48]

The lessons garnered from the dying enrich life with meaning. Their influence can be profound. A dying professor, Morrie Schwartz, shared this insight with his former student Mitch Albom.

"Everyone knows they're going to die," offered Morrie, "but nobody believes it. If we did, we would do things differently."[49]

Blessed with this deepened perspective, we might contemplate that very thought: how we might do things differently. The topic is a common assignment for writing students, one that is worded something like this: *If you knew that tomorrow was to be the last day of your life, how would you spend it? What would you do from the moment you awakened until you turned off the last light at night?* The question is not a new one, but it is relevant, because it opens a window into the heart.

The answers are as varied as they are revealing, especially in their simplicity. They often include spending time with someone cherished. Or enjoying something we typically deny ourselves: calorie-laden treats or an afternoon walk in the park. Or savoring a more appreciative look at that which we take for granted: a sunset, a tree-lined path in the forest. Or solidifying a treasured relationship by asking forgiveness or expressing love. The question is worth pondering, because in doing so we may hear God's whispers; we may understand the actions He would have us take *now* rather than waiting until it is too late.

Upon surviving a loss, our pacing with life as we knew it may strike us as out of sync. We depart from the hospital or funeral home, confronted by the reality that the lives of others are proceeding in the same manner that they were when we first entered the inner sanctum of sorrow. This catches us off guard. To others, nothing has changed. People clutching briefcases still race along sidewalks. Horns honk. Grocery clerks look bored, oblivious to the enormity of our pain. Suddenly life takes on unfamiliar shapes like the melting clocks in a Salvador Dali painting.

If loss has left us lonely or alone, time may seem to have stretched a few sizes too big, and it feels as if we are swimming in it. If, through our loss, existing responsibilities take a back seat to new ones, such as executing a will or caring for a widowed parent, time may seem as if it has shrunk, perhaps to a size that is so tight, it may feel suffocating.

The pain is deep, and for some it is hard to see beyond loss. Others may hurry through, unconsciously distracting themselves in an attempt to keep grief at bay. But God is patient and compassionate, an unassuming gift-giver. Without our realizing it, perhaps God's gift will emanate from the very loneliness of loss, eventually leading to the discovery of relationships that may have otherwise gone unrevealed. Or maybe an overwhelmed state will lead to the seeking of quiet, unveiling the richness of time spent in solitude.

The dignity with which my father faced death was undeniable. At the end of his life, he made the most of his time, encouraged others and avoided self-pity, consistent with actions his whole life long. Still, it took a while before I would ponder the potential relevance of these qualities to my own life. After Dad died, I mourned, of course. Yet, in some way, I think the subsequent busying of myself was a smokescreen for the intensity of my grief.

I'd cared for Dad in his final weeks, and now a new chapter was about to begin: caring for my eighty-six-year-old mother who was nearly deaf and entering the dark halls of dementia. Soon I was swimming in a sea of overwhelming responsibility.

With Dad gone, my dining room table became a repository for the new life awaiting me, which included many of the personal, legal, financial and medical tasks to which my father had once tended. On the table were piles of bank and investment statements, notes from conversations with estate lawyers and accountants, utility bills from my parents' Florida condo, the paperwork for getting Mother moved to Lancaster—utilities hook-up forms, apartment leases, a scattering of medical and Social Security records. I dived into these new efforts, while attempting to continue my obligations as mother, wife, the financial manager of my husband's graphic design business and my own writing career, not to mention various volunteer commitments. I was swamped and, I must admit, not handling the pressure well.

Rob Bell writes of the need "to remind myself that I did not make the world and that it will continue to exist without my efforts."[50] That sentence is underlined in my copy of his book, a star drawn next to it.

I made trips to Florida to gather Mother's belongings, to meet with lawyers, to empty the condo and get it ready to sell. At the same time, her moves here in Lancaster had to be orchestrated. And moves there were—eventually, five of them through the continuing care continuum—none of which Mother herself relished, of course. Burdening her daughters was never her intention.

Nonetheless, I started feeling imposed upon. My shoulders began to hurt. My husband would forget to fill out his time sheet, preventing me from completing his bookkeeping, and he may as well have gone out dancing in blatant disregard of my overwhelmed state. Or Mother would mention a need for hearing aid batteries, and it would feel as though she'd asked me to make a side trip to Zimbawe.

Finally, a nudging inside (which I now perceive as the Holy Spirit) urged me to take a reprieve, and through the grace of God, I heeded. With my family's blessing, I packed a suitcase and drove to a nearby spiritual retreat center where unbeknownst to me, I would spend a weekend listening to the gentle voice of God. To greet me, a sign hung beside the front desk. It resonated with me because in all my busyness, I had barely acknowledged God. The sign quoted Hilary Ottenmeyer, O.S.B.: "Until you are convinced that prayer is the best use of your time, you won't find time for prayer."

Then I checked into room #410 and put down my suitcase. There on the bulletin board to welcome me were the words of Blessed Therese de Soubiran.

"O richness of the present moment
you are infinite
since you contain my God!
Why not love you?
Why not enclose myself
entirely in you?"

It seemed that from the moment I stepped into the

retreat center, God was waiting for me, open-armed. *What took you so long? Welcome. Here, let me show you the way.* God was present for me in nature. He was there in the books that I read. He was shining a light on the notebook I brought in which to write. God's presence was so comforting, I felt myself settling into His embrace.

And so I started to notice things that seemed to be put there for my benefit. Out my bedroom window, the perfect rows of farmland. A white house in the distance with black shutters. A hopeful sky tinged with pink. Laughter. People arriving for a weekend of prayer and fellowship. The kaleidoscopic autumn trees lining a path where I walked. The sun rising behind a field of wheat. A patch of yellow flowers. A waterfall gushing over boulders. Two bushel baskets of leaves, a rake nearby.

In the retreat center's bookstore, a little book called *Slow Down Therapy* caught my eye, so I bought it and took it back to my room.

"Direct your life with purposeful choices, not with speed and efficiency," one page offered. "The best musician is one who plays with expression and meaning, not the one who finishes first."[51]

It was like being in a conversation directly with God.

"I hear you," I would say.

And then God would speak again, through rays of

sunlight on my window sill, through signs hanging on the elevator walls, through a Bible study workbook I'd brought along, through a tiny nun in the dining room who pointed at the salad bar sprouts and, in a thick Italian accent, asked me, "Whatsa that?" Stop. Take notice. How nice of God to theme the weekend for me. To remind me what it felt like to laugh. In a book called *Soul Gardening*, an Alice Walker quote called my name. "If you pass by the color purple in a field and don't notice it," Walker asserts, "God gets real pissed off."

That weekend, one of the first times since Dad's illness and death that I'd offered God my undivided attention, I was lavished with sacred gifts. I was reminded of the reasons to relinquish control and let God take charge. Looking back, I recognized the path on which God had led me; the markers along the way started to make sense, as they had guided me to exactly where I was at that point in time. And looking forward, I saw new possibilities for my faith, for my family, for my relationships and for my work. Better ways to allocate my time that might enrich the rest of the ride. I was filled with hope. Amazing. And grace.

Slowing down to hear God's voice is a lesson I have learned again and again. It is probably the lesson that has had the most profound effect on my life (and His patience in repeatedly and gently revealing the exact same material truly touches me). For in spending time with God, my heart is comforted and more clearly focused. I gain strength to face new challenges. And my spirit is buoyed by His love.

The lessons you learn—whatever they may be—can lead you to make the most of your time here on earth. They may help you to face adversity, to slow down or they may provide one of hundreds of other insights. But one thing is certain: God uses our losses to help us. What an honor it is to the memory of those we have lost to embrace the gifts that God offers on their behalf.

For Writing and Reflection

Reflect on a life lesson learned through loss. How might it enrich the rest of your days here on earth?

"How lucky I am to have

known someone who was so hard

to say good-bye to."

Winnie the Pooh

nine
embraced by
gratitude

twenty
great years

O ne of my favorite forms of prayer is a gratitude list that I keep on my computer. It is simply a laundry list of things for which I am grateful, and every time that I go to it and add a few more items, it reminds me of how much God loves me. The list is nothing extraordinary, but to me, the sum of the parts—such as my husband's Chinese chicken salad, books to read, the walking paths through Landis Woods—fills me with the warmth of God's grace.

Gratitude comforts. Gratitude heals. When we think of those we have lost with gratitude for who they were and for what they meant to us—and even for the ways we have grown through loss—God's love embraces us. As John of the Cross said, "One act of thanksgiving made when things go wrong is worth a thousand when things go well."

Recently I met a young woman whose baby girl had

died at twenty-one days old. The doctors had predicted the child would barely survive childbirth, and when she did, they affirmed their prognosis that death was imminent. Each day the parents woke up expecting their precious daughter might die. Their grief was overwhelming, day after day after day. Finally, the couple decided to focus on the things in life for which they were grateful. They began to keep a gratitude list, and in doing so, they embraced a perspective that got them through each day, feeling God's love and able to celebrate their newborn child's life, as short as it was.

The stories I received from those so generous to share their loss experiences for this book were imbued with gratitude. For some, this sense was so powerful that the thankfulness itself was a gift of comfort. The following is a gratitude list of a special type. It is a mosaic of some of the expressions of gratitude that I've had the privilege of reading in my research for this book. They're from people who have lost so much, yet miraculously feel compelled to embrace their blessings. I hope they inspire you, as they have me.

Jim, who lost his ninety-four-year-old mother:

"It was never a matter of obligation to include her in our activities. She was fun to be around and made everything more

enjoyable. She was outgoing, the consummate storyteller, and had a great sense of humor. And she was always a role model— we all learned from her whether it was family values, manners, entertaining, cooking or kindness to others.

"Do we all miss her greatly? Yes. Is there ever a day we don't think about her? No. But I can't say we're grieving. Rather we feel so fortunate to have had such a long, happy and close relationship with her."

A friend's cousin who lost her son in a freak accident on the soccer field:

On the drive to her son's funeral service, the mother tried to gather her thoughts. She wanted to say something at the service in honor of her twenty-year-old son, but she could not find the words. What would her message be? Then a billboard she passed inspired the answer to her quandary. The advertiser was a local heating and plumbing company that was going out of business. The words on the billboard: *Thanks for twenty great years.*

Zenta, upon losing her father:

"He was truly a one of a kind. He was beloved in so many areas, it's mind-boggling. I very much feel his presence and positive energy every day. He inspires me more now than ever."

C.S. Lewis, who lost his wife:

"Praise is the mode of love which always has some element of joy in it. Praise in due order; of Him as the giver, of her as the gift… by praising I can still, in some degree, enjoy her, and already, in some degree enjoy Him. Better than nothing."[52]

Mike and Brie, who lost their four-hour-old baby:

Brie: *"He had a sweet disposition. He was a great baby."*

Mike (pointing to a page in a photo album from Luke's short life): *"The picture of him smiling there—that is what we experienced."*

Sandy, who lost her father:

"I miss Dad. When I think of him, I do not think of him as dead…I visualize him serving God in heaven with more gusto and joy than ever!"

Peter, who cherishes the memory of one of his last visits with his grandfather:

"He stood as a silhouette on the front porch, waving to me as I drove away. He looked like an angel with the porch lamp outlining him on a warm July night."

Pam, who lost her father:

"He was the most joyous and most despondent man I knew,

possessing more character in his femur than some people accrued over a lifetime. He was both vice and virtue—a self-contained yin and yang— a pure divine spark of God's light and dark....Few men had the wit, the intellect and dead-on observational qualities of my father. He could read people like they came with instructions, a quality I unfortunately did not inherit..."

Elizabeth Edwards, who lost her sixteen-year-old son in a car accident:

"I have sometimes talked about the strange gift that comes with the awful tragedy of losing a child. I had already been through the worst, I believed; we all had, and I had the gift of knowing that nothing will ever be as bad as that. The worst day of my life had already come."[53]

Betsy, who lost her father:

"My father was very sweet to me. You know, you stand on your father's shiny shoes and dance. I remember horseplay with him, being on his back and he on his hands and knees. He was the one person who could really make me laugh."

Deb, who lost her father:

"My father was always a selfless, generous man his whole life, and he showed that until the very end."

Ann Hood, who lost her five-year-old daughter:

"It has been three years since Grace died. My husband has turned fifty since then. He is a handsome man, but sorrow has taken some of the twinkle from his eyes. He is a man who believes in the power of church and religion. He wants a simple thing: for his wife and his son to stand beside him and lift their voices in a song of gratitude for what we have and for having had Grace at all. I try to give him this. It isn't easy, but I am trying."[54]

For Writing & Reflection

Write a Gratitude List, a long one. List one-hundred things for which you are grateful. Consider keeping the list going, adding new entries day after day.

"… the Father of compassion and the God of all comfort….comforts us in all our troubles, so that we can comfort those in any trouble with the comfort we ourselves have received from God."

2 Corinthians 1:4

ten

embraced by community

little band of
mourners

They have been referred to as my little band of mourners. My healing force. Angels from God. You may know them simply as friends. Or family.

"I called them my posse, because they protected me from threats to my equilibrium" writes Lyz Glick of those who comforted her after the death of her husband Jeremy on United Airlines Flight 93, September 11, 2001. "My posse was with me almost constantly in the days immediately following the disaster."[55]

These are the people who stop what they are doing to join us on sorrow's path. They ask for nothing; they simply reach out with acts of love, soothing words, affirmation or practical assistance. They represent humanity at its best, stepping forward to help fulfill one of God's promises, as stated in the Old Testament: "Never will I leave you; never will I forsake you."[56]

Some are blessed with community, embracing it as a

lifeline through grief. Others long for such a gift and, in its absence, may seek for and discover alternatives.

My neighbor Beth's eyes light up as she speaks of those she's dubbed "my little band of mourners." A retired teacher who lives alone, Beth returned home after dark one mid-summer evening to find calling cards from the local police tucked into the crevices of all her doors. On the cards, scribbled in large black letters, were the words, CALL ASAP. Scared that she had done something wrong— had she unknowingly run over something?—Beth would soon learn that her eighty-two-year-old father, recently diagnosed with depression, had "decided that he was just too lonely; he couldn't do this any longer." The loss was devastating.

Beth called out to God in the middle of the night. She felt helpless. She felt angry. "Help me know what to do," she pleaded.

The answer to her prayer came in the form of people —many people, she asserts—joining her on her path.

"And they wouldn't just *be* on the path," she remembers. "They'd come up and walk with me along the path." Some were people she met for the first time—parishioners from her father's church, the attorney, office secretaries— and others were her own siblings, their spouses and family members arriving from out of town, as well as friends.

One was the associate pastor from her father's church, a woman she had never before met. Beth recalls her first meeting with Cathy.

"I can tell you exactly what she had on when I first saw her in my living room. She is my rock. She is my source of peace. In the midst of horror, deep grief, confusion, exhaustion…she brought peace. It's just her demeanor. She's tall and broad-shouldered and she stood in front of me, and she went like this," remembers Beth, opening her arms. "And she said, 'You must be Beth.' And with that, I was in her arms."

One Sunday when she visited Cathy's church, Beth arrived to discover that she and Cathy were wearing outfits cut of the same fabric. Later, after she started attending Cathy's church, Beth would view this occurrence as God's way of helping her see herself at home here.

"God has a sense of humor, and he's steadfast," says Beth. "His presence can be so incredibly steadfast through the people who are around us if we take the time to see it, to acknowledge it and embrace it. And I had to; I had to. For my health and if I'm going to contribute in life, then I had to."

The manifestations of grace during her time of anguish and pain remain vivid in Beth's mind, continuing to comfort her.

"When I think of the long hours during those first days spent on my porch, I see only the love and care we had for each other," she recalls. "I see my cousin Jim and his wife on that first evening, my elderly aunts and uncles who sat quietly, not knowing what to say. My sister, nephew, brother-in-law sat out there through the dark hours of night. I see all the church folk who knew to come around the house to the porch when no one answered the front door. There were so many people, and the gifts each brought were concern and abiding love. Those memories will encourage me forever."

> ## God's presence can be so incredibly steadfast through the people who are around us ...
>
> —Beth

Beth asserts that "even in the darkest moments and most painful throes of grief, each of us is capable of hearing the music of care, reassurance, steadfast presence and peace that is offered by the people who surround us....If we listen and open our eyes and hearts, even when exhausted and blinded by tears, those gifts of loving care will…sustain our spirits."

For those like Beth who live alone, this appearance of others "coming up over the ridge and walking with us," as Beth described, is especially significant.

My friend Steven, an entrepreneur who also lives alone, had always shared a fiery but close relationship with his mother. When she died, just months after his father's death, Steven was deeply moved by the support he received from friends.

"I don't have a family," he explains. "My closest friends are my family. The night she died, as soon as I got home, there were people there waiting. *They* are my home. I felt lifted…I really felt how much love I have in my life. Being alone is not necessarily lonely. The outpouring of love from people was more overwhelming to me than my mother's death."

The opportunity to share grief may present itself unexpectedly, some-

> "
> The outpouring of love from people was more overwhelming to me than my mother's death.
>
> **—Steven**
> "

times through one individual, even a stranger. Suddenly someone—a compassionate someone—appears and, out of his or her own experience, provides an understanding that only those arising from the darkness themselves can offer.

In a lecture entitled "Give Sorrow Words," author and Vermont College of Fine Arts faculty member Chris Noël speaks of such a person.

"One-hundred-and-thirty-three days ago, I went to pick my father up at the Burlington Airport; he didn't get off the plane because he had, a day earlier, dropped dead of a heart attack, by himself, in his Santa Barbara apartment, having had no symptoms and a cholesterol level of 174.

"A few days after Daniel Noël died, I got a Federal Express delivery. Brian, the driver, could plainly see I'd been crying, so I told him what had happened, and he didn't flinch. His own father had died three years ago, and he stood with me for forty minutes recalling episodes of strange and comforting connection with his dad during the first few months. When I said I was about to fly to California to deal with the apartment and other logistics, Brian gave me the following advice: 'This is going to sound really weird, but I'd tell you to *savor* it.' I hugged the man, and then flew this phrase as my personal banner during the whole laborious process in Santa Barbara. My sister Becky and I could tell from some dried vomit on the rug where Dad had lain down. After packing the place up and cleaning for three days, she and I each took a last turn in the apartment alone. I took off all my clothes and lay down where he had, and felt the absolute dependence of infancy."

The chance to express feelings honestly to one who will listen without judging is one of the finest gifts one human being can offer another, especially in the face of grief. Those on the receiving end will vouch for the healing this act of love promotes.

When Mike and Bric learned that their unborn son had a fatal condition called Ellis Von Crebil Disease, "there was a lot of sadness," Mike remembers. "We shed a lot of tears. I don't know that it was daily, but probably pretty close. Our family and friends really helped a lot through that time. We had a lot of support. You experience God's grace through his people."

At first, when the couple was offered the services of a hospital chaplain whose job it is to help families like theirs through the grief process, Mike and Bric were hesitant.

"We weren't trying to be arrogant or proud, but we felt that with our family and our church family, we would be well supported," Mike admits. "We thought the hospital chaplain was more for people without support."

Then they met Carolanne. A blonde woman with blue eyes, she greeted the couple warmly.

"She was like an angel sent from above," Brie says. "Very gentle and understanding, sincere."

"It was like God had designed her for this role," Mike adds, "the way she expressed her sadness for what we were going through. And the questions she asked that helped us look within ourselves."

"She asked direct questions about how this was affecting our faith, what were our feelings toward God," Brie recalls. "She allowed us to be honest. It was a safe place to be honest."

"There was nothing we could say that would change her view of us," Mike asserts. As the day of Luke's birth approached, Carolanne supported the couple by assembling a hospital team, answering questions, and helping them think about the process and what to expect. She even prayed with them.

> **She was like an angel sent from above.**
>
> —Brie

Finally, Luke was born, a precious and beautiful baby. Family and friends gathered at the hospital, holding and getting to know him. As they experienced an outpouring of love for their newborn son, relationships that were already strong felt even stronger. All too soon, Luke's four short hours of life drew to a close, and the couple asked to be alone with him. Afterwards, they kept him in the room with them for the duration of their hospital stay.

"For someone looking in," says Brie, "they may think it's weird that you have your dead child in the bassinette next to you, but to us, it felt right."

"We didn't plan for that," adds Mike. "Even though his body was there and his spirit had left and there was no life there, we still wanted to keep him covered with the blanket and make sure that he was snuggled. There was still that nurturing aspect. We wanted to be sure he was okay. That was part of our healing. We would hold him periodically."

When Carolanne entered the room, she gave Luke a kiss on the cheek and picked him up.

"Those were the things that made us feel that he was valued as a person, even after he was gone," Mike says. "And that helped a lot. It helped a lot."

Those blessed to experience this brand of affirmation receive more comfort from it than those extending it might guess. For when we lose someone we love, the realization that his or her life touched others, as well, not only affirms our own feelings but acknowledges our loved one as a precious child of God.

When Zenta's father died, the response of others whose lives he had touched imbued her grieving with an unexpected richness.

"I had no idea he had this impact on others," she wrote to me in an email. "To me he was just Dad, a great dad who had an impact on *me*. But I never had a clue his influence was so wide-ranging."

As the days and weeks after his death passed, Zenta kept me apprised of her experience.

"It's as if a rock star died," she wrote shortly after the memorial service. "I've been fielding emails and letters and calls all week…The impact my father had on people was profound."

Zenta emailed me photos from the memorial service, newspaper tributes written about her father and messages received from people who had known him.

"Of course, as daughters, we love, adore and lift our own fathers up," she wrote, "but when we see others do the same (or dare even more), it is so affirming."

This affirmation arrives in many forms. Whether it is a kind word, a loving action or an offer of help, the soothing offered by others is an intangible gift whose long-lasting effect cannot be overestimated.

Eleven years after her husband of thirty-five years died, a woman named Norma recalls the glimmers of hope that helped her through her loss. Among them were "the faces of my three beautiful sons...my friends and family. But of the many wonderful things that were said to me during my time of grieving, the one thing that my friend Joanne said to me was something of comfort that I still carry with me today:'Joe O'Brien was proud to have you on his arm.'"

It may feel awkward to some well-wishers, not knowing exactly what to say or do, but the effort made—in whatever sincere form—can be a blessing for mourners. My friend Howard's experience with a young Amish woman soon after the shooting of ten Amish girls in a one-room Lancaster County schoolhouse illustrates the point.

Like many of us who live in the area, upon hearing the tragic news, Howard felt sympathy for the victims' families and for the Amish community as a whole. The day after the tragedy, I received this email from him.

"As you may know, I go to the nearby Farmer's Market, and as you probably also know, most of the booths are run by Amish folks. It would be a stretch to say that over the years I've gotten to know a few of them, because they are very private people, but with one or two there has been more than passing contact.

"Such is the case with a young woman—maybe 20 or so, hard to tell—who works in a pie/cake/doughnut booth. We have at least chatted a little.

"I knew today I couldn't go in with business as usual. So I was starting to say, 'I know that at a time like this words are meaningless, but…'

"And before I could go on, she looked me right in the eyes and said, 'Words are never meaningless.'"

Indeed.

Certainly all survivors do not experience this reaching out. In fact, in contrast, loss leaves many alone and lonely. Even those who experience an initial swell of sympathy may feel forgotten as friends and relatives retreat, often not knowing how to help, or simply returning to their own busy lives and failing to follow up. I must admit my personal failure in this regard; certainly after more than one funeral, distracted by the demands of my own routine, I have neglected to pick up the phone and call.

Because of age or other isolating circumstances, there may be no "posse" of supporters to gather around, few well-wishers extending words of comfort. Elderly people who are widowed and childless, for example, may face unwelcome days and weeks of solitude. Instead of sensing others coming up on the path to join them, they may be challenged to venture onto side paths to discover community on their own, daring themselves to branch out in exploration.

When Bea Decker's husband, Bob, died unexpectedly, she clung to the words he had spoken, almost prophetically, just days before his unexpected death.

"The real Christian meets the test when things go wrong," Bob had said, "and he still maintains that God is a good and loving God."[57]

With Bob's words resonating in her mind, and in his honor, Bea used the grief and solitude she experienced to create a group called THEOS (They Help Each Other Spiritually), "a nationally known organization of widowed men and women who face the problems and challenges of their situations together."

Others seek out support groups, join activities, discover new hobbies, or decide to turn lonely hours into volunteer efforts.

"If you truly want to find joy again," offered one THEOS program speaker, "try giving yourself away. The important thing is that you are giving, not thinking of getting. If you...start...even a tiny bit, the world will observe your spirit and throw many opportunities for giving at your doorstep. And there will be return—far greater from giving than getting."[58]

Whether we have been blessed by compassionate support or simply wished that we had, we can use our experience—our knowledge of what it feels like to lose someone we love—to extend God's grace to others.

It is illuminating to sit in a room full of hospice volunteer trainees, for example. The trainer suggests that we go around the room stating our names and the reason behind the decision to volunteer for hospice. The most common answer goes something like this: "Hospice was there for us when I lost my [fill in the blank—mother, father, husband, wife, brother, sister]…and now I feel compelled to give something back." Or, "We called hospice too late, and wished we'd had their support sooner."

> ## If you truly want to find joy again, try giving yourself away.
> —Rev. Paul Gerhard

One after another, you can see it in their eyes; these people have been there. Many have agonized through the nightly vigils. Others have been jolted awake by the early morning phone call. Some have rubbed weakened shoulders, deteriorating backs. Many have shed more tears than they'd realize they were capable of producing. And through it, they were somehow touched by the presence of others. Now they intend to extend the very same grace so lovingly shown them.

Through my volunteer service with hospice, I see this all the time. I've also seen it in the shaping of this book. People digging deep into their own experiences and reaching out in the chance that their stories might offer hope to others.

"If a few hearts can resonate with mine," writes author Gordon Livingston, whose six-year-old son died of leukemia, "perhaps we can share an understanding of what it means to love, to grieve, to be human...."[59]

I wonder if this is all part of God's plan. Pass it on, *pay it forward*: you've heard it expressed before. God's loving grace embraces us in our sorrow and, in turn, we can extend it to others.

"At times, there was a lot of anger with God about the fact that this is too much," Beth recalls about her father's suicide. "But I can tell you two-and-a-half years later, as difficult as it all was, if I'm to give thanks, it is for the ability to look at someone else, not that I can say I understand, but I can say 'You need time and you need loving care. And I can give you both. And other people can give you both.'"

As heart-wrenching as was the loss of their infant son, Mike and Brie agree.

"We can see things God has done in our lives," Mike says, "drawing us closer to Him and together in our marriage, even opportunities we've had with other people who have gone through periods of pain. We are able to express ourselves in a way we wouldn't have been able to before. When I see someone going through a difficult experience I can empathize in a way I couldn't before.

"We both are so blessed," Mike elaborates. "We both had a wonderful childhood and great families. Our parents are together. Our parents have functionally healthy homes. We've had it easy, the cookie-cutter-American life. And everything was perfect with Colson. It was the way we thought life was supposed to go.

"I remember hearing this about grief, that one day you wake up and you're in unfamiliar territory. You're like, 'Is this my life? This isn't what I expected life to be.' You're still on the journey, but you're on a different road, and you don't recognize where you are. We felt like that a lot of times.

"We've been able to express to people in a more understanding way when they're going through painful times because we've experienced pain."

"It's created a depth within us that wasn't there before,"

adds Brie.

"I've learned to give people space and time to grieve, to not give answers, to be there for them," says Mike. "And I think we tend to be more proactive to show that we care, not just asking if there's anything we can do."

"When you're in the midst of grieving you really don't know what you need," explains Brie. "You're just trying to get through moment by moment, just trying to hold it together to get through the day."

"Even if someone asked, 'Would it help if I did *this*?' That was really helpful. I could say yes or no," recalls Mike. "The more specific the better."

They remember the offers to clean their house, the donation of Luke's burial spot, the meals that were brought, the babysitting assistance with their two-year-old son, Colson. In November, a couple of months after the burial, Mike and Brie got away on a trip to Aruba—just the two of them—and while they were gone, both of their mothers snuck over to their house and planted tulips.

"In the spring, tulips started popping up," Brie says, "yellow, and pink and white—these beautiful colors. At Easter, my mother told us they'd planted them in memory of Luke. Such an act of love toward us."

This is the love that emanates from God. Magnificent and yet just a hint of the abundance with which God intends to shower us. We can only imagine how it might touch us in another configuration of time, in the moment of reunion. That is, I believe, the supreme grace of God: the hope of eternal life.

A time will come in your mourning when you will feel able to light another's candle. It may not be today or next week or even next year. But whenever it occurs and in whatever the way, you will likely recognize the nudge. Perhaps an obituary photo will stir you. Or an unexpected encounter. Or tears shed by someone you know. The embrace of grace. It is yours to receive. And, whenever the time is appropriate, it may also be yours to deliver.

For Writing & Reflection

Recall the comfort you received or wished you had received from others as you grieved. Based on your own experience, list those gestures that you might offer others who find themselves in similar situations.

afterword

I t was a cloudy July afternoon in the summer of 2000,
another season of sadness. Sand oozed through my
toes as I maneuvered around the debris left by a
storm on Lighthouse Beach. We had come to Cape Cod
because my husband and I had planned this trip long before Dad was pronounced terminally ill, and Dad insisted
I take a reprieve from worrying about him. At the time, he
had not yet moved into the sunroom of my home where
he would spend his final nine days, but the leukemia was
robbing me of the father I adored; that much was certain.

Now as the waves crashed against the shore, I pondered
how others fared through the loss of someone they'd loved
so intensely. I needed to know this. I longed to hear the
voices of those who had so sharply grieved similar depths
of loss. As time went on, I became one of these voices,
because in living with loss and in discovering the other
side of grief, I wanted to illuminate it. Soon I encoun-

tered others compelled to share the hope they'd found, as well.

As C. S. Lewis notes, "I have been emboldened to write of it because I notice that a man seldom mentions what he had supposed to be his most idiosyncratic sensations without receiving from at least one (often more) of those present, "What! Have you felt that too? I always thought I was the only one."[60]

Gifts of grace continue to touch me. As I shared early drafts of this book's manuscript, I was inspired in unexpected ways by the people who had read it. For not only did they offer valuable feedback on the work itself, but in many cases, the reader shared with me a personal experience of loss in which he or she had discovered grace. Because I received their stories before publication, some of them have been woven into these pages, and the book is stronger because of them.

Since you are reading this book, I would venture to guess that, in some way, you are dealing with the profound absence of a loved one. And I wonder if, amidst the emptiness, you have ever felt the embrace of grace. Perhaps you, too, after reading the stories of others, are moved to share one of your own.

If so, I invite you to visit www.aswegrieve.com where there is a menu item entitled "Readers' Voices." Please feel free to click on that heading and add your voice to those of others who, amidst their deepest losses, have found hope. Or you may choose to share your story in a support group, on a note card, on the telephone, over a cup of tea or to simply listen when others wish to share.

On that long-ago-summer day on Lighthouse Beach, the wondering began. *What do others feel like? How do they get through?* Like the rippling waves not far from shore, patterns of grace—my own and those of others—would soon reveal themselves. What a rich gift it has been to feel the blessing of kinship along the walk.

J.G.
Lititz, PA

notes

CHAPTER ONE: EMBRACED BY GRACE

1   Chad Walsh, afterword, *A Grief Observed*, by C. S. Lewis
    (New York: Bantam, 1976) 113.
2   James 1:17.
3   John Claypool, *Tracks of a Fellow Struggler* (Waco, Texas: Word
    Incorporated, 1974) 54.
4   Isaiah 40:31
5   Claypool 57–58.
6   Gerald L. Sittser, *A Grace Disguised* (Grand Rapids, Michigan:
    Zondervan Publishing, 1995) 43.
7   Toby Talbot, *A Book About My Mother* (New York: Farrar,
    Straus and Giroux, 1980) 16.

CHAPTER TWO: EMBRACED BY DISCOVERY

8   Parker J. Palmer, *Let Your Life Speak* (San Francisco: Jossey-
    Bass, 2000) 54.
9   Patrice Gaines, *Moments of Grace: Meeting the Challenge to
    Change* (New York: Three Rivers Press, 1997) 21.
10 David Treadway, *Dead Reckoning: A Therapist Confronts His
    Own Grief* (New York: BasicBooks, 1996) 247.
11 Maggie Callanan, *Final Journeys: A Practical Guide for Bringing
    Care and Comfort at the End of Life* (New York: Bantam Dell,
    2008) 135.

CHAPTER THREE: EMBRACED BY MEMORIES

12 Sittser 60.
13 Nancy Cobb, *In Lieu of Flowers* (New York: Pantheon, 2000)
    53.

14   Gaines 1.
15   Gaines 22.
16   Tall Rock Retreat About Us Page, 2007-2008, Christopher
     Noël. 13 October, 2008.
     http.//www.tallrockretreat.com/History___Future.html

CHAPTER FOUR: EMBRACED BY HUMOR
17   Allen Klein, "Grief Relief: Looking for Laughter in Loss,"
     Self Improvement Online, Inc., May 12, 2007
     http://www.SelfGrowth.com
18   DeWitt Henry, Sorrow's Company (Boston: Beacon Press,
     2001) XII.
19   Henry XIII
20   Cobb 58.
21   Alexandra Shulman. "A Shoe With a View." First published in
     British Vogue, July 1994, ©Condé Nast Publications. Manolo
     Blahník, Manolo Blahník: Drawings (New York: Thames &
     Hudson, 2003) 158.
22   Allen Klein, The Courage to Laugh: Humor, Hope, and Healing
     in the Face of Death and Dying (New York: Tarcher/Putnam,
     1998) 43.
23   Klein 64.
24   Ecclesiastes 3:4
25   Klein 399.

CHAPTER FIVE: EMBRACED BY STRENGTH
26   1 Samuel 17:33
27   Samuel Lee Oliver, MDiv, BCC, What the Dying Teach Us:
     Lessons on Living (Binghamton, NY: The Haworth Press,
     1998) 106.
28   Sameet M Kumar, Ph.D., Grieving Mindfully (Oakland, Cali-
     fornia: New Harbinger Publications, 2005) 118.
29   Callanan 18-19.

30   Oliver 21.

31   Proverbs 3:5-6

CHAPTER SIX: EMBRACED BY FAITH

32   Isaiah 9:2

33   Oliver 59.

34   Oliver 65.

35   Oswald Chambers, *My Utmost for His Highest* (Grand Rapids, Michigan: Discovery House Publishers, 1992) February 10.

CHAPTER SEVEN: EMBRACED BY ART

36   Sandra L. Bertman, PhD., ed., *Grief and the Healing Arts: Creativity as Therapy* (Amityville, New York: Baywood Publishing Company, 1999) 7.

37   Madeleine L'Engle, *Walking on Water: Reflections on Faith and Art* (Colorado Springs, Colorado: Waterbrook Press, 2001) 57.

38   Jan Groft, *Riding the Dog: My Father's Journey Home* (Grand Rapids, Michigan: Faithwalk, 2004) 1.

39   Joy S. Berger, *Music of the Soul: Composing Life Out of Loss* (New York: Taylor & Francis Group, 2006) 3.

40   Cobb 11.

41   Martha Whitmore Hackman, *Healing after Loss: Daily Meditations for Working through Grief* (New York: Harper Collins, 1994) January 12.

42   Henriette Anne Klauser, PhD., *With Pen in Hand: The Healing Power of Writing* (Cambridge, Massachusetts: 2003) 3.

43   Klauser 10 (italics mine).

44   Kay Gibbons, "My Mother, Literature, and a Life Split Neatly into Two Halves," *The Writer on Her Work*, Volume II, ed. Janet Sternburg (New York: Norton, 1991) 52.

45   William Loizeaux, *Anna: A Daughter's Life* (New York: Arcade Publishing, 1993) ix.

46   Groft 155.

CHAPTER EIGHT: EMBRACED BY WISDOM
47   Sittser 36.
48   Anne Lamott, "The View from Here," *O, The Oprah Magazine,*
     Oct. 2003, Vol. 4, Issue 10, 208.
49   Mitch Albom, *Tuesdays with Morrie* (New York: Doubleday,
     1997) 81.
50   Rob Bell, *Velvet Elvis* (Grand Rapids, Michigan: Zondervan,
     2005) 117.
51   Linus Mundy, *Slow-down Therapy* (St. Meinrad, Indiana: Abbey
     Press, 1990) 25.

CHAPTER NINE: EMBRACED BY GRATITUDE
52   C. S. Lewis, *A Grief Observed* (New York: Bantam, 1976) 72.
53   Elizabeth Edwards, *Saving Graces* (New York: Broadway
     Books, 2006) 18.
54   Ann Hood, *Comfort* (New York: W. W. Norton & Company,
     2008) 131.

CHAPTER TEN: EMBRACED BY COMMUNITY
55   Lyz Glick and Dan Zegart, *Your Father's Voice* (New York: St.
     Martin's Press, 2004) 22.
56   Hebrews 13:5
57   Bea Decker, as told to Gladys Kooiman, *After the Flowers Have
     Gone* (Grand Rapids, Michigan: Zondervan, 1973) 170.
58   Decker 170.
59   Gordon Livingston, "Only Spring," *Sorrow's Company*. Ed.
     Dewitt Henry (Boston: Beacon Press, 2001) xix.

AFTERWORD
60   C. S. Lewis, *Surprised by Joy* (New York: Harcourt, Brace and
     Company, 1955) vii.

To post your own discovery of grace in grief, please visit www.aswegrieve.com.